Chinese Foreign Policy after the Cultural Revolution, 1966-1977

Other Titles in This Series

Westview Special Studies on China and East Asia

Chinese Foreign Policy after the Cultural Revolution, 1966-1977
Robert G. Sutter

Chinese foreign policy has changed radically since the Cultural Revolution of 1966-1969, but until now there has been no comprehensive review of developments in Chinese foreign affairs over the past ten years. Robert Sutter, making extensive use of recently declassified U.S. government reports, focuses on turning points in China's policy and analyzes the reasons for Peking's policy choices. Dr. Sutter looks at the influence of foreign pressures on China and assesses the impact of ongoing internal political struggles on the conduct of Chinese foreign affairs. His conclusions offer insights into the implications of the purge of four leftist Chinese Politburo members following the death of Mao Tse-tung in September 1976.

Written for both the China specialist and the general reader, this book presents first an overview of the course of Chinese foreign policy during the decade, and then a detailed examination of Chinese policy on significant foreign issues. The result is a rare and authoritative guide to scholars and others interested in recent developments in China and other communist-ruled states.

Robert G. Sutter, an Asian affairs analyst with the Congressional Research Service of the Library of Congress, also teaches East Asian history at the University of Virginia, Falls Church. From 1968 through February 1977 Dr. Sutter was a Chinese foreign policy analyst with the Central Intelligence Agency.

Chinese Foreign Policy after the Cultural Revolution, 1966-1977

Robert G. Sutter

Westview Press • Boulder, Colorado

0736531
8440

Westview Special Studies on China and East Asia

Copyright © 1978 by Westview Press

Published in 1978 in the United States of America by
  Westview Press, Inc.
  5500 Central Avenue
  Boulder, Colorado 80301
  Frederick A. Praeger, Published and Editorial Director

Library of Congress Cataloging in Publication Data
Sutter, Robert G
  Chinese foreign policy after the cultural revolution.
  (Westview special studies on China and East Asia)
  1. China—Foreign relations—1949-1976. I. Title.

DS777.55.S88   327.51   77.7018

ISBN 0-89158-342-4

Printed and bound in the United States of America

Contents

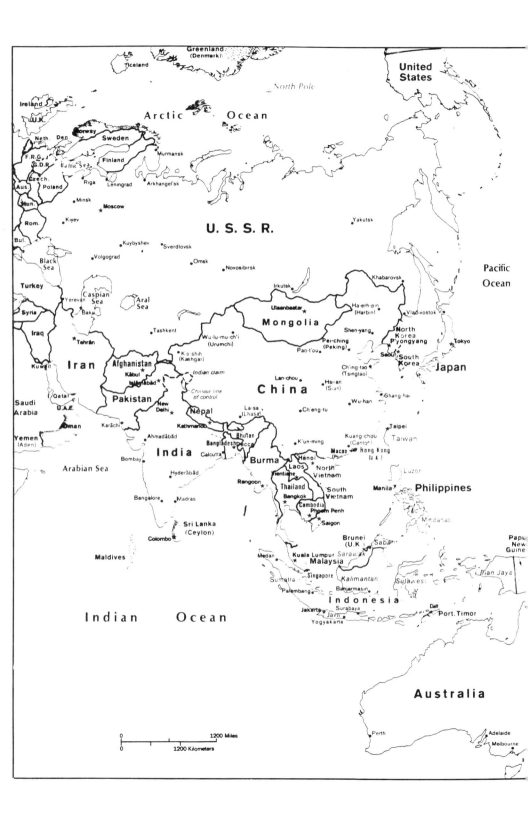

Preface

At the urging of Frederick A. Praeger, I agreed to write a brief study of Chinese foreign policy since the Cultural Revolution. There seemed to be a need for a book that would review, summarize, and analyze the significant developments in recent Chinese foreign affairs, both for the China specialist and for the interested reader.

The result is the following study, which is divided into two parts. Part One provides an analysis of the major turning points in the development of recent Chinese foreign policy. Part Two gives greater attention to Peking's policies toward particular countries, regions, and issues important to China. The two parts are designed to complement one another, but they can also be used separately. Thus, for example, a general reader who is interested only in a brief review of Chinese foreign policy might confine his or her reading to Part One; a specialist keenly interested in China's relations with the USSR might want to turn immediately to the section in Part Two dealing with Sino-Soviet relations.

Footnotes have not been used since sources are cited throughout the body of the study. A major aid in the writing of the book was the recently declassified series of weekly reports on Chinese and other communist countries' media pronouncements, which are published by the U.S. government's Foreign Broadcast Information Service under the titles *Trends in Communist Propaganda* and *Trends in Communist Media*. These reports are now declassified six months after the date of issue and are available for sale to the public. They are a rare, authoritative guide to scholars and others interested in recent events in China and other communist states.

Robert G. Sutter

Abbreviations

ANZUS	Australia–New Zealand–U.S. Security Treaty
ASEAN	Association of Southeast Asian Nations
CCP	Chinese Communist Party
CPSU	Communist Party of the Soviet Union
CSCE	Conference on Security and Cooperation in Europe
DPRK	Democratic People's Republic of Korea
DRV	Democratic Republic of Vietnam
FRG	Federal Republic of Germany
JSP	Japanese Socialist Party
KCNA	Korean Central News Agency
KWP	Korean Workers' Party
MCP	Malaysian Communist Party
NCNA	New China News Agency
NPC	National People's Congress
PCI	Italian Communist Party
PLA	People's Liberation Army
PRC	People's Republic of China
ROC	Republic of China
SEATO	Southeast Asian Treaty Organization
UAR	United Arab Republic
VOMR	Voice of the Malayan Revolution
VOPB	Voice of the People of Burma
VOPT	Voice of the People of Thailand
VWP	Vietnamese Workers' Party
WDC	World Disarmament Conference

Chinese Foreign Policy after the Cultural Revolution, 1966-1977

Part One

The Evolution of Chinese Foreign Policy, 1966-1977

Introduction

Peking's foreign policy has been designed on the one hand to guarantee the development and advancement of China's vital interests in world affairs, and on the other hand to spread Maoist ideology and world revolution. The vital interests of the People's Republic of China (PRC) in international affairs center on the following points:

- Peking is anxious to obtain and consolidate control over regions that traditionally have been subject to Chinese rule. Taiwan is a notable example.
- Peking seeks to develop an independent and strong position in world affairs, free from the dominance of outside powers.
- Peking strives to develop its wealth and power to the

point where China will be able to reattain its historical-
ly influential position in East Asian politics.

Peking's leaders have long realized that a pragmatic
approach to foreign affairs, devoid of ideological encum-
brances, has provided the most efficient way for the PRC to
secure its national interests. However, these same leaders
have remained committed to Maoist ideology and have
promoted the spread of international communist revolution. This situation has led to a continuing contradiction—
and a source of dynamism—in Chinese foreign policy. The
interaction and frequent conflicts between the pursuit of
China's vital interests and the concurrent drive for world
revolution have given Chinese foreign policy an unpredicta-
ble changeable quality.

Two other sources of change in Chinese foreign policy
have been the influence both of PRC internal politics and of
international politics. Thus, for example, revelations of
PRC leadership upheavals since the start of the Cultural
Revolution in the mid-1960s have made it clear that Chinese
internal politics sometimes have had a major impact in PRC
foreign affairs. On the other hand, the influence of the U.S.
containment policy against China in the 1950s and the
impact of Soviet pressure on China during recent years
underline the frequently heavy impact of international
politics on the conduct of PRC foreign policy.

PRC foreign policy up to 1958 was influenced primarily
by international pressures on China. The start of the Cold
War and the buildup of U.S. strategic power in East Asia
prompted the Chinese to move closer to their ideological
allies in the USSR—leading to the establishment of the Sino-
Soviet alliance in 1950. The new ties with the USSR provided the PRC with a necessary strategic guarantee of
security in the face of the major threat Peking saw posed by

the United States. They also gave Peking a source of supplies for modernization, as the USSR began to transfer technological expertise and economic assistance to China.

Following the Korean War, Peking's foreign perspective became dominated by a growing concern over the U.S. strategic network in East Asia designed to "contain" Chinese influence. U.S. military forces were reinforced throughout the region, and Washington began establishing bilateral and multilateral pacts with a number of noncommunist Asian states. In the face of the growing menace it saw posed by U.S. containment, Peking looked to its Soviet ally for increased support. It found Moscow—in the wake of Stalin's death— decidedly less interested in supporting China against the United States in East Asia. Moscow was now stressing Soviet desire for peaceful coexistence with the United States, especially in Europe. It showed little interest in backing efforts by China which risked confrontation with the United States in East Asia.

Judging that the use of force against the United States would be foolhardy unless they were sure of strong Soviet support, the Chinese chose to seek negotiations with the United States. Meeting with the United States for two years during bilateral ambassadorial-level negotiations in Geneva, Chinese representatives strove to find a common ground. However, the negotiations proved fruitless, in large part because of U.S. determination not to compromise with the PRC.

Soviet rocket successes of late 1957 brought about an apparent change in Peking's view of the international balance of power, which in turn prompted a shift in PRC foreign policy. Peking now saw Moscow as strengthened vis-à-vis the United States and tried to elicit greater Soviet support for PRC objectives blocked by U.S. containment in East Asia. This policy failed during the 1958 Taiwan straits crisis: Moscow only belatedly supported China in the face of a strong U.S. response to the PRC blockade of off-shore islands held by Taipei.

Over the next ten years, Peking came to see international politics and the balance of power in East Asia as relatively stable. Peking continued to strongly oppose the United States, and it also began increasingly virulent polemics against its former ally, the USSR. The Chinese apparently judged that they now could afford to alienate both super-powers, since neither the United States nor the Soviet Union showed signs of significantly endangering PRC national security. For example, the USSR acted to insure that its polemics with China would not lead to an open military conflict, and the United States carefully reassured China regarding U.S. intentions following the escalation of U.S. military involvement in Indochina.

It was during this ten-year period—from 1959 to 1969—that PRC internal politics and leadership disputes appeared to play a pivotal role in the conduct of PRC foreign policy. Not faced with an immediate threat to their security, the Chinese could afford to allow their foreign policy to be influenced significantly by factors other than the need to secure national defense and strategic safety. In particular, leadership power struggles and domestic disruptions during the 1966-1969 Cultural Revolution brought normal PRC foreign policy functioning to a halt. Senior Chinese diplomats were recalled to China and junior officers remaining overseas were required to proselytize in the name of Mao Tse-tung. Rigidly ideological conduct in foreign affairs was the order of the day, leading to a severe downturn in Chinese relations with a large number of previously friendly states. This resulted in increasing PRC diplomatic isolation, to a point where China's circle of foreign friends was limited to Albania, Pakistan, and a handful of African states.

Over the next several years—1969-1976—Chinese foreign policy returned to a more pragmatic, conventional diplomatic approach better designed to protect and strengthen China's vital interests in the East Asian balance of power. A sharp change in the strategic balance during the late 1960s— brought on most notably by the rapid growth of Soviet power along the Sino-Soviet frontier—was responsible for this shift toward pragmatism and moderation in Chinese foreign affairs. In this context, PRC internal politics and leadership disputes came to play an increasingly less important role in Chinese foreign policy. Thus, the past ten years can be viewed as a progression from a period when PRC internal politics and Maoist ideology were dominant influences to a time when international pressures on China and a pragmatic approach to world affairs became the overriding features of Chinese foreign policy.

Early Efforts To Resume Normal Diplomacy, 1968

As the Cultural Revolution drew to a close in 1968, Chinese foreign policy was only beginning to emerge from the disruption and disorganization caused by the previous three years of leadership purges and strident support for Maoist ideology and insurrection abroad. Red Guard demonstrations against foreign installations in China had been halted, and Chinese officials had begun efforts to restore diplomatic functioning with a few, selected third world states.

Peking's limited resumption of normal diplomacy was well illustrated by its differing approach to third world states during mid-1968. At that time, a succession of official visitors to China indicated an effort on the part of the PRC to reduce its isolation in foreign affairs while striking a more careful balance between the politics of Maoist insurrection and conventional diplomacy. Visits to the PRC by a joint

Guinean-Malian foreign ministers' delegation, a Malian military delegation, and President Nyerere of Tanzania gave Peking an opportunity to bolster its footholds in Africa and undertake a diplomatic offensive with offers of aid and support in the name of Afro-Asian unity in opposition to imperialism. While Peking predictably used the Africans' visits to play up the antiimperialist line, the Chinese at the same time sought to refurbish their image in a less radical context by paying renewed homage to peaceful coexistence—a theme which emerged with notable prominence during the visit in late May of the Nepalese deputy prime minister.

The emerging trend toward normalization of the PRC's foreign affairs introduced a more orderly arrangement in Peking's dealings with the external world. However, Peking's hard line toward the United States and the Soviet Union remained intact, along with continued pressure on regimes of the third world regarded as pawns in a Soviet-U.S. attempt to contain China within a hostile environment. Regimes in the latter category included India and Burma, which continued to be the targets of propaganda attacks and PRC-supported, Maoist-style people's wars.

The vist of Deputy Prime Minister Bista of Nepal in 1968 afforded Peking an opportunity to demonstrate a desire for normal relations with a regime sharing a minimum of China's revolutionary interests. The joint communiqué issued on 1 June reflected a prominent theme of the visit in registering satisfaction with the development of friendly relations based on "the five principles of peaceful coexistence." The communiqué noted that a new trade agreement had been reached and that the PRC offered to extend increased economic aid to Nepal. On foreign affairs matters, however, the communiqué simply noted that the two sides had exchanged views on questions of common interest.

Unlike recent radical African visitors to China, Bista did not favor his hosts with endorsements of Chinese revolutionary aims or of the Cultural Revolution, generally limiting himself to words of appreciation for PRC economic aid and for the "correct and friendly" manner in which Nepal had been treated. Such remarks and the invocation of the five principles reflected a mutual desire to remove the strains resulting from the troubles of the previous summer, when Maoist evangelism had spilled over into Nepal and stirred up local sensitivities. During the visit the Chinese did, however, inject elements of their own particular orientation, as on 24 May when Foreign Minister Chen I at a banquet described friendly relations between the two countries as an example of the five principles and a contribution to Afro-Asian unity against imperialism.

Several days after Bista's visit, at a Nepalese embassy reception on 11 June celebrating King Mahendra's birthday, Chen I gave a blatantly tendentious reading of the five principles in a context clearly aimed at India. After claiming that the Chinese under Mao "first initiated and consistently carried out" the five principles of peaceful coexistence, Chen assailed "certain people" for "feverishly tailing after imperialism and modern revisionism" in vilifying China and attempting to form an anti-China alliance. He added that the unnamed Indians had discarded the five principles of peaceful coexistence which they had once supported. Peking's revival of the Bandung spirit thus proceeded in a selective manner.

Underlining its selective approach to third world nations, Peking continued its severe pressure on India, both as a rival for Asian power whose interests were regarded as inimical to those of China and as a prime target for Peking's insurrectionary line. Chinese propaganda pounded away at the growing relations between the Soviets and India in the wake of Premier Kosygin's visit to India in early 1968, and persistently offered evidence of Indian involvement in alleged Soviet and American efforts at forging a ring of encirclement to contain Chinese influence. Thus a New China News Agency (NCNA) report on 8 June, discussing Mrs. Gandhi's tour of Australia, New Zealand, and Malaysia that spring, charged that she had discarded Nehru's "phony" stance of nonalignment and had openly engaged in efforts to further plans by Washington and Moscow to set up an anti-China alliance in Asia.

On the insurrectionary front, Chinese propaganda sought to encourage peasant insurgencies and armed uprisings by dissident minorities in India. Thus a 15 June NCNA dispatch took note of the serious clashes which erupted a week earlier between Naga guerrillas and Indian government forces. The dispatch, which referred to "courageous resistance" by Naga and Mizo armed forces "struggling for national liberation," did not acknowledge Indian charges that the insurgents were trained and supplied by the Chinese. A protest lodged by India on 19 June accused the PRC of complicity in aiding subversive elements in northeastern India.

As in the case of India, Peking continued to give low-level publicity to subversive actions in Burma by communists and dissident minority groups. A roundup of reported actions issued by Peking on 11 June mentioned the armed forces of the pro-Peking Burmese communists, various nationality groups, and the National Democratic United Front engaged in sabotage activities against the "reactionary" Burmese government. Chinese propaganda also attacked the Burmese regime for allegedly collaborating with Thailand and India in efforts to suppress the "people's armed forces" operating in the three countries. On 14 June NCNA quoted the insurrectionary "Voice of the People of Thailand" transmitter which denounced the "Thanom-Praphat traitorous clique" and the "Ne Win reactionary clique" for having agreed the previous month to join in subduing the rebels. A similar theme had been played by Peking regarding the Nagas at the time of Ne Win's visit to India in March.

Impact of Soviet Pressure, 1968-1969

Peking's efforts in conventional diplomacy did not begin to pick up steam until Chinese leaders became aware of the serious international pressures on China in the late 1960s. China was in a particularly weak and vulnerable position, in part because its military forces had become bogged down in domestic chores involving the maintenance of order and management of civilian administrative affairs. At the same time, the Brezhnev leadership had begun a largescale build-up of Soviet forces along the Sino-Soviet frontier, to a point where Moscow had the capability of striking deeply into China along most sections of the border.

Peking did not show an awareness of the serious weakness of its position vis-à-vis the USSR until after the August 1968 Soviet invasion of Czechoslovakia. The Soviet action and its justification in terms of the so-called Brezhnev doctrine of limited sovereignty served notice to Peking that Moscow might be inclined to use its strategic advantage against China just as it had against Czechoslovakia. In response, Peking for the first time began to protest alleged Soviet intrusions along the Sino-Soviet border. It also took several steps to broaden China's heretofore limited circle of foreign friends—trying in this way to improve PRC international leverage against the USSR. In particular, Peking moved quickly to solidify its relations with Albania and Romania, and began efforts to patch up its strained ties with France and Yugoslavia. The Chinese also showed signs of a thaw in Sino-Vietnamese relations, which had been particularly cool following Hanoi's decision to disregard Peking's advice and enter into negotiations with the United States in Paris in May 1968.

The most notable feature of the newly moderate Chinese approach to foreign affairs was the Chinese foreign ministry spokesman's unusually mildly worded statement of 26 November 1968 proposing the reconvention of the Warsaw ambassadorial talks with the United States on 20 February 1969. The initiative—timed to coincide with the coming to power of the Nixon administration—was closely associated with Premier Chou En-lai. Chou presumably judged that improved relations with the United States would serve to offset the Soviet pressure on China. Peking also appeared interested in sounding out the new U.S. administration— which was urging broad cutbacks in U.S. commitments abroad—over its intentions toward China.

Chou's initiative soon ran into opposition from leftists in the PRC leadership, who argued that it was improper for China to negotiate with a major enemy such as the United States. While they did not explicitly attack Chou's initiative, the leftists sponsored a media line opposing the use of negotiations in dealing with the United States. They eventually won over the majority of the Chinese leadership, forcing the cancellation of the scheduled Sino-U.S. meeting in Warsaw, using as a pretext the U.S. role in the early 1969 defection of the PRC chargé d'affaires in the Netherlands.

Over the next eight months, Peking did little to develop a pragmatic approach in foreign affairs. Although China was preoccupied with the Soviet threat following the March 1969 outbreak of armed border clashes along the Manchurian frontier, the Chinese continued to rebuff the overtures of the Nixon administration. Chou En-lai and other advocates of a more pragmatic Chinese foreign policy were blocked by leftist Chinese Politburo members headed by Chiang Ching, who presumably had the backing of Chou's major rival for power in the Chinese leadership—Defense Minister Lin Piao.

As a result of the leadership impasse, little progress was made in efforts toward normalization in PRC foreign policy. In May 1969, Peking announced the start of restaffing of the ambassadorial posts left vacant during the Cultural Revolution. On the 15th Peking stated that Keng Piao had been appointed ambassador to Albania, and on 20 May it reported that Huang Chen was returning to his post in France. These moves toward more conventional diplomacy had been presaged on May Day, when Mao Tse-tung had made a point of receiving eight newly accredited ambassadors to the PRC.

Meanwhile, Peking showed some signs of a more active role in Eastern Europe. NCNA on 31 May announced the departure of a PRC foreign trade delegation to Romania and Czechoslovakia. On 22 May, the Polish press agency reported the arrival of a PRC trade delegation for talks on an agreement for 1969. These were the first Chinese trade delegations to go to Eastern Europe since the advent of the Cultural Revolution. On 8 May Peking sent a message greeting the Czech Government on Czechoslovakia's national day—the first such Chinese message to a Soviet bloc nation in over a year.

Such small gestures did little to improve China's weakness and isolation before the Soviet Union, however. Serious clashes along the Sino-Soviet frontier and an escalation in threatening Soviet propaganda during August finally prompted a change in Chinese policy. Intensified Soviet pressure set the stage for talks at the Peking airport on 11 September 1969 between Kosygin and Chou En-lai. Soviet pressure forced the Chinese leaders to disavow their previous ideologically based opposition to talks with "imperialist" enemies such as the United States and the Soviet Union, and marked the beginning of an increasingly pragmatic Chinese approach to foreign affairs.

It was clear that Peking could no longer stridently oppose Moscow over the border problem. Under the guidance of Chou En-lai, Peking compromised and agreed to start negotiations in order to defuse the border crisis and guarantee Chinese national security. However, Peking's move came only after apparently heated debate and behind-the-scenes bargaining within the Chinese leadership. After Kosygin made an offer for border talks on 11 September, the Chinese waited almost a month before announcing their acceptance on 7 October. The talks began on 20 October, but were accompanied by media commentaries (associated with the leftists) that voiced opposition to negotiations with the Soviet Union. As in the case of leftist-inspired commentaries criticizing Chou's initiative towards the United States in late 1968, the current commentaries did not explicitly attack the border talks with the USSR, but made clear an opposition to the principle of using negotiations in dealing with major enemies like the United States and the Soviet Union.

In contrast to a year earlier, Chou and his allies were able to weather this opposition from the leftists; the talks with the Soviets proceeded on schedule. Peking's comments made it clear that while China was willing to meet the Soviet representatives in talks to ease tensions, China's fundamental opposition to the Soviet Union had not changed. In fact, Chou En-lai capitalized on his success in bringing about the Sino-Soviet talks to begin an unprecedented, pragmatic PRC foreign policy effort designed to enhance China's international leverage against what Peking now saw as its major enemy—the USSR. This Chouist approach was to dominate Chinese foreign policy in the 1970s.

Chou En-lai's Efforts To Increase PRC
International Leverage, 1969-1970

Chou En-lai acted first of all to improve China's strained relations with its Asian communist neighbors, North Vietnam and North Korea. Relations with Hanoi showed improvement following the warm Chinese welcome which greeted the visits of Premier Pham Van Dong of the Democratic Republic of Vietnam (DRV) in October 1969 and of a South Vietnamese communist delegation the following month. Peking commentary and reportage once again began to actively support Hanoi's war effort, and Peking—for the first time—endorsed the Vietnamese communists' position in the Paris peace talks with the United States.

The development of China's relations with North Korea was even more striking, culminating in Chou En-lai's 5-7 April 1970 visit to the Democratic People's Republic of Korea (DPRK). Chou's stay in Pyongyang capped a warming trend in Sino-Korean relations which began following the start—in September 1969—of Chou's active role in developing a pragmatic approach in PRC foreign affairs. Kim Il-sung and Chou had talks on 5 and 6 April which both sides described as "cordial and friendly." Chou's activities in Pyongyang included attending banquets on 6 and 7 April and addressing a city meeting on 7th. At the banquet on the 7th, Kim said the two leaders had reached a "complete unanimity of view," and in his departure speech at the airport that day Chou pointed to the "very fruitful results" of the visit. Reports and speeches on both sides stressed the close friendship of the two peoples, "sealed in blood," and recalled that Chinese volunteers had participated in the Korean War.

Speeches made by Kim and Chou during the visit underlined a need for greater unity between their countries in the

face of allegedly intensified U.S. and Japanese aggressive-
ness in Asia. The tone was set in the arrival speeches at the
airport on the 5th. Welcoming Chou, Kim stressed that the
people of the two countries are "close comrades-in-arms and
brothers fighting shoulder to shoulder against the common
enemies—Japanese militarism and U.S. imperialism." He
asserted that a "tense situation" had been created in Asia as a
result of aggressive U.S. and Japanese moves and that
Chou's visit "at this juncture is an event of great significance." In reply, Chou declared that relations between the
Chinese and Koreans are "like lips and teeth," and that their
peoples are "intimate brothers." He recalled that the two
nations had fought shoulder to shoulder against the United
States and Japan. He stated that in conditions in which the
United States and Japan were intensifying aggression
against China, Korea, the "three countries of Indochina,"
and other Asian countries, the strengthening of Chinese and
Korean unity was "of great significance."

Though Peking's rivalry with Moscow was not emphasized during Chou's visit, Chinese resentment over Soviet
dealings with Japan—expressed in a 31 March 1970 NCNA
charge that Moscow had sold out Soviet sovereignty by
granting Siberian air rights to Japan—was reflected in
Chou's assertion on 5 April that the attitude taken toward
Japan was an important criterion for distinguishing between "genuine and sham" revolution, socialism, and
Marxism-Leninism. Having thus used language reminis-
cent of Peking's ideological contest with Moscow, Chou
sought to associate Pyongyang with this view, quoting the
North Koreans as having said the same thing in their
statement that one's position on Japan "is a question of
fundamental stand."

Chou returned to this theme, with its clear anti-Soviet
overtones, in his speech on the 7th in which he complained

that "some people talk about opposing imperialism" but are actually conducting "an ardent flirtation" with the United States and Japan. Chou thus managed skillfully to exploit a matter of mutual concern to Peking and Pyongyang, serving Peking's interests both in breaking out of its isolation and in securing an important flank in its contention with the Soviets. Though Pyongyang sedulously avoided being identified with either side in the Sino-Soviet conflict, Chou's visit underscored a convergence of interest between Peking and Pyongyang in opposition to Soviet aims in the area.

Other manifestations of Chinese flexibility at this time were seen in China's relations with Yugoslavia and Egypt. Earlier signs that Sino-Yugoslav relations had improved were confirmed in a Yuvoslav foreign ministry spokesman's announcement on 20 November 1969 that Peking and Belgrade—after an 11 year hiatus—had agreed in principle to resume diplomatic relations at the ambassadorial level. The Chinese decision to normalize diplomatic ties with Yugoslavia not only reflected Peking's efforts to break out of its previous diplomatic isolation but underlined China's special interest in seeking leverage in Eastern Europe—an area extremely sensitive for Soviet interests. Meanwhile, Chou En-lai on 2 February 1970 issued a message to Nasser, marking the first such official Chinese statement of support for the Arabs to be publicized by the Peking media since the June 1967 war. NCNA reported on 2 February that Chou received the United Arab Republic (UAR) ambassador that day and during a "cordial and friendly talk" handed him a letter for Nasser expressing the Chinese people's concern for the Arab struggle and pledging to remain "the most reliable friend" of the people of Egypt, Palestine, and the other Arab countries.

By far the most important change in China's posture at this time was Peking's revival of a moderate approach toward the United States—a policy which culminated in Chinese agreement to resume the ambassadorial-level talks in Warsaw in January 1970. Peking's continued concern over Soviet pressure, its persistent worry over Soviet-U.S. "collusion" against Chinese international interests, and its preoccupation with gaining foreign leverage against the Soviet Union at this time all set the stage for China's attempt to strengthen its position vis-à-vis the Soviet Union through utilization of its relationship with the United States.

The revival of the ambassadorial talks had quick impact on the USSR. Moscow media began to note the serious implications for Soviet interests stemming from a possible rapprochement in Sino-American relations. The United States, of course, was encouraged by Peking's response. It continued to initiate policy designed to bring about an easing of the Sino-U.S. confrontation in East Asia.

By spring 1970, Peking had successfully begun a pragmatic and moderate policy in foreign affairs that had significantly altered China's previously weak position in international affairs. Although the Sino-Soviet talks made no progress, they had defused the border crisis. Under the cover of a large-scale Chinese domestic campaign to "prepare for war," the Chinese had also begun a longterm effort to bring their military power up to high standards, especially in regions along the Sino-Soviet border. Armed forces previously used to protect southern and eastern China against an attack from the United States were transferred northward to positions for defense against the USSR.

Peking had achieved important breakthroughs in its relations with strategic communist, third world, and capitalist states. The new Chinese openness toward the United States—seen in the revived Warsaw talks—gave special reassurance to China. In particular, Moscow's show of irritation over the Sino-U.S. talks demonstrated to Peking that the USSR was not sure what the U.S. response would be in the event of a Soviet incursion into China or a major Sino-Soviet war.

China's new confidence over its international position was reflected in an unlikely vehicle—Mao's 20 May 1970 statement condemning the United States for its invasion of Cambodia. Peking had informed the United States two days earlier that China was suspending the Sino-U.S. talks as a result of U.S. actions in Cambodia. By this time, Peking felt confident enough about its security to temporarily sever its public link with the United States. Peking showed its new confidence by altering its propaganda line about the danger of war, especially a war involving China. Previously, Chinese comment had been equivocal over whether "war" or "revolution" was the dominant trend in world politics, and had warned particularly about the danger of a war breaking out which would eventually involve China. In contrast, Mao's 20 May 1970 statement for the first time downgraded the danger of war against China and claimed emphatically that "revolution" was the "main trend."

Peking's Line against the Superpowers, 1970-1973

Reflecting China's new confidence, Chou En-lai set forth the centerpiece of Peking's new line in foreign affairs in 1970. Chou claimed that China should now strive to form a broad united front with all countries against the two "superpowers." In a symbolic gesture, Chou initiated his new line during an interview with French newsmen on 14 July—the national day of France, the prime example of a Western country which had opposed the "domination" of both the United States and the Soviet Union. NCNA replayed Chou's interview on 28 July.

According to NCNA, Chou observed that there are "one or two superpowers" which seek to bully the weak as part of their rivalry for world hegemony. He paraphrased Mao's 20 May 1970 statement in noting that the danger that the big powers might launch a world war still existed, but he reflected genuine confidence—in contrast to Chinese expressions reflecting PRC isolation and concern during the past year—in asserting that times had changed and the days when the big powers decided the world destiny were over.

Peking propaganda quickly adopted Chou's antisuperpower line as the major theme in Chinese foreign affairs in the 1970s. However, it became increasingly clear that Peking was using the antisuperpower line primarily against the Soviet Union, and that the United States was receiving a relatively mild treatment by Chinese media. In particular, the United States was repeatedly portrayed as a declining power with whom Peking could negotiate and compromise as part of China's efforts to offset the power of its main adversary, the USSR.

Not only did Chinese propaganda see the United States as less of a threat, but it also began to respond with increasing interest to the Nixon administration's repeated calls for improved relations. Thus, for example, even though the Chinese suspended the Warsaw talks on 18 May 1970, Peking began secret correspondence with the Nixon administration. The impact of this effort was not publicly noted until Chou En-lai received a U.S. ping-pong team in Peking during April 1971. At the same time, U.S. journalist Edgar Snow revealed that Mao had expressed an interest in having Nixon visit China. This set the stage for Dr. Kissinger's secret trip to Peking in July 1971 to make arrangements for the president's visit.

In contrast, Peking showed little interest in rapprochement with the Soviet Union. Chinese negotiators maintained an intransigent position in the Peking border talks. Although the Chinese agreed to renew trade ties and ambassadorial level relations with Moscow, PRC propaganda made it clear that Peking had not altered its strong, anti-Soviet bias.

A prime example of Peking's increasingly differentiated approach toward the two superpowers was seen in Chinese propaganda regarding Western Europe. Consistent with Chou's July 1970 remarks criticizing both superpowers, Peking media at first favored resistance by Western European countries against both the United States and the Soviet Union, claiming that Europe would not be secure until the NATO and Warsaw Pact military alliances were destroyed. As China gradually placed more trust in the United States' ability to act as a counterweight against the Soviet Union, Peking media adopted an approach that softened criticism of the United States while playing up the need for Western Europeans to resist the USSR. In particular, Peking came to support closer Western European cooperation with the United States against the Soviet "threat." It implicitly supported a U.S. military presence in Europe while endeavoring to foment resistance to Soviet "domination."

Reflecting its interest in early 1972 in capitalizing on trends favorable to China's rivalry with the two superpowers, especially the Soviet Union, Peking played up the development of Western European nations into a more closely unified force capable of challenging Soviet and American dominance in Europe. Chinese comment directed favorable attention to the trend toward broader representation within the European Community, encouraging the Common Market states to heighten coordination not only in economic matters but also in political and foreign affairs.

Underlining Peking's more positive approach, NCNA's detailed and favorable account on 26 January 1972 of the entry of Britain and three other nations into the Common Market demonstrated several departures from Peking's previous assessments of Common Market developments. Where Peking had previously focused on persisting conflicts of interest among Western European states as evidence of the overall decline of the world capitalist system, the 26 January NCNA account took the line that pressures from the Soviet Union and the United States had caused a "realignment" among European capitalist states, forcing them to put aside differences in order to defend mutual interests against outside dominance. Peking had habitually depicted the Common Market as a tool of oppression against the European working class by capitalist rulers, but the NCNA report all but ignored this ideological theme.

Reflecting a reduced concern over the United States as a threat to the PRC's international positions and a growing interest in checking Soviet influence, Peking shifted from its former portrayal of Western European unity as directed chiefly against Washington and lauded the virtues of unity vis-à-vis both the Soviet Union and the United States. Thus, while citing Britain's entry into the Common Market as signaling the end of the British-U.S. "special relationship" and marking the further decline of U.S. influence abroad, Chinese comment took care to remind the Europeans that Soviet pressure became an increasing concern as U.S. presence declined.

Viewing political consolidation as an effective counterweight to Soviet and U.S. influence, the 26 January NCNA account pointedly quoted statements by European spokesmen such as Chancellor Brandt of the Federal Republic of Germany (FRG) and Common Market President Malfatti calling for closer political and economic ties within the group. The account indicated that the planned Common Market summit conference for that year would be significant for future coordination in political and foreign affairs.

By early 1973, Peking media had begun to imply support

for an active U.S. role in Europe. Reflecting its more relaxed stance toward U.S. military policy following Nixon's visit to China and its increasingly evident concern to encourage a strong American military presence in Europe to counterbalance Soviet power, Peking reacted to Secretary Laird's annual defense report to Congress with a low-level NCNA account on 11 January—carried only in the agency's domestic service—that ignored U.S. policy in Asia while highlighting the secretary's call for a strong U.S. defense posture together with enhanced Western European capabilities. While observing that the United States "will continue its arms race with another superpower," NCNA avoided the sharply critical comment that had marked Peking's reaction to the previous year's defense report.

Commentary in 1972 had placed heaviest stress on U.S. military strategy along China's periphery in Asia, noting that the Laird report's statements concerning the use of indigenous Asian forces and the encouragement of the modernization of Japanese military forces could not but arouse the Chinese to "high vigilance and firm opposition." As in the 1972 commentary, Peking in 1973 briefly noted recent U.S.-Soviet agreements, including the SALT and Berlin accords and movement toward a European security conference and talks on balanced force reduction in Europe, but 1972 charges of Soviet-U.S. "collusion" were notably absent. Peking also muted stress in 1972 on U.S. difficulties with major European allies while citing the secretary's appeal for the Western Europeans to make a greater contribution to allied strength.

In keeping with Peking's line that recent trends toward Soviet-U.S. and European détente were deceptive and masked Moscow's expansionist urges, NCNA quoted Secretary Laird's admonition against lowering the West's guard and his observation that profound differences still existed between the two blocs. NCNA also cited his reference to Soviet naval expansion, and it took care to quote his remarks on the complexity of the question of balanced force reduction in Europe. In discussing the appeal for the Western European countries to assume a greater defense role, NCNA cited the Laird report as stressing that the United States would continue to shoulder the major responsibility for the allied nuclear deterrent and would continue massive contributions to the alliance's conventional military forces. The NCNA account concluded by noting, with implicit satisfaction, that Defense Secretary–designate Richardson had voiced similar views in testimony to a Senate committee on 9 January.

Peking's treatment of the Laird report comported with other signs pointing to a concern with encouraging a continued American presence in Europe as a counterweight to the Soviets. Peking's line had stressed the need for European unity and independence vis-à-vis the two superpowers, but this approach was now offset to some measure by Peking's overriding interest in promoting countervailing forces against the Soviets. Thus, NCNA's 16 December 1972 report on the first session of the preparatory talks on European security pointed out Romania's assertion of independence in demanding an equal voice for all states despite their alliance affiliations, and similarly noted Western European objections to the Brezhnev doctrine; however, NCNA soft-pedaled criticism of American dominance in Western Europe while taking note of the U.S. representative's assertion that Europe's security was indivisible from that of the United States. Earlier, an 11 December 1972 NCNA account of the NATO ministerial meeting gave top billing to U.S. statements at the session, including a letter from President Nixon pointing to a need for continued NATO military preparedness despite prospects for détente and pledging that the United States would maintain its forces in Europe. NCNA also quoted Secretary Rogers to the effect that NATO must remain wary of any attempt by Moscow to use the European security conference to confirm its hegemony in Eastern Europe. An NCNA dispatch datelined Bonn on 10 January 1973 reported the NATO military maneuvers that began the day before and pointedly quoted a commentary in a West German paper as saying that the presence of American troops in Europe was important for the FRG.

Peking's altered approach was also reflected in its coverage of Common Market developments. In keeping with a shift from the former portrayal of the Common Market as an instrument for asserting Western European independence of American control, Peking began favoring British rather than French spokesmen in conveying Chinese attitudes toward Western European developments. Where the French had long voiced views that served Peking's interest in fostering independence of the two superpowers, the British were now being cited as favoring continued close ties with the United States. Thus, NCNA's 4 January 1973 account of Prime Minister Heath's remarks on British accession to the Common Market quoted him as saying that Europe should seek to be a "valid partner" of the United States while striving to develop its own strength.

Impact of the Paris Peace Agreement, 1973

The January 1973 Paris agreement, which called a halt to the Vietnam war and mandated a U.S. military withdrawal from Vietnam, served to enhance Peking's differentiated approach toward the two superpowers. Chinese propaganda indicated that the peace settlement had reassured China over U.S. intentions in East Asia by removing one of the major irritants in Sino-U.S. relations. The agreement opened the way for improvement in Sino-U.S. relations while fostering greater Chinese confidence in its own strategic position in the East Asian balance of power.

An accelerated momentum in Sino-U.S. relations was registered in the 22 February 1973 communiqué on Dr. Kissinger's 15-19 February visit to China, which came significantly during the period when Peking had welcomed the Vietnam agreement as conducive to détente in Asia. Consistent with its increasingly clear willingness to accept a continuing American presence in East Asia in the terms of the Nixon Doctrine, Peking largely avoided criticism of the instruments of the U.S. presence: the mutual security treaty with Japan, SEATO, the network of U.S. bases along China's flanks, and other former targets of Chinese denunciation. At the same time, Peking took a relaxed posture toward Taiwan, making a pitch to nationalistic sentiment on the island while pointedly citing President Nixon's trip to Peking as a sign of the new times.

Promptly capitalizing on the improved atmosphere produced by the Vietnam accord, Peking was extraordinarily forthcoming in its treatment of Kissinger's visit. Most notably, Peking's highest sanction was conveyed by Mao's meeting with Kissinger, an honor that in the recent past had been accorded only to heads of state and foreign ministers. The point was brought further home in NCNA's account of the "frank and wideranging conversation in an unconstrained atmosphere," in which Mao asked Kissinger to "convey his regards to President Nixon."

In warmly welcoming the Vietnam agreement, Peking expressed relief that an encumbrance on Sino-U.S. relations had been removed—a reaction reflected in the statement in the communiqué on Kissinger's visit that "the time was appropriate" for accelerating the normalization of relations. Peking was cautious about placing responsibility on the United States for alleged violations of the Paris agreement. In an authoritative comment on the subject, a 15 February article appearing in *People's Daily* under the byline "Commentator" seconding Vietnamese communist protests made only passing mention of a U.S. responsibility for "enjoining" Saigon to comply with the provisions of the agreement. A 23 February *People's Daily* editorial hailing the signing of the Paris agreement regarding a peace settlement in Laos mildly urged the United States to observe the terms of the accord by withdrawing its military personnel and terminating all military activities in Laos.

Peking's first direct reference to a continuing U.S. involvement in Thailand following the signing of the Vietnam agreement appeared—without comment—in a 14 February NCNA report on the U.S. announcement two days earlier that the headquarters of American air operations in Southeast Asia would be transferred from South Vietnam to Thailand. A 23 February NCNA account of a Philippine Communist Party statement welcoming the Vietnam agreement quoted the statement as warning the Vietnamese to remain vigilant so long as the United States maintained military bases and troops in Indochina, and "in neighboring countries like the Philippines, Thailand, and other Asian countries." However, Peking's replays of statements on the Vietnam agreement from other Maoist Southeast Asian parties carefully sanitized criticism of the United States as well as of Southeast Asian governments. NCNA's report of a Thai Communist Party congratulatory statement to the Vietnamese communists deleted a passage that described the United States as "brutal, ferocious, extremely arrogant, and economically and militarily powerful," as well as one that called for a protracted Thai people's war to "drive out U.S. imperialists and overthrow the reactionary Thanom clique."

Peking's more moderate treatment of the U.S. role in Asia was accompanied by a more relaxed and sophisticated propaganda effort toward the people on Taiwan in an attempt to capitalize on the PRC's improved international position as well as to stimulate a sense of Chinese national unity and patriotism. This effort followed lines established over the previous year in inviting Chinese to visit the mainland and underscoring Peking's concern for the "compatriots" on Taiwan; the propaganda fare was enriched by the use of spokesmen who enjoyed greater credibility and respect on Taiwan, by more varied and attractive programming, and by attempts to achieve a greater impact on Taiwan from the breakthroughs in the PRC's relations with the United States and Japan.

An outstanding example of this enrichment was a talk by Chinese philosopher Feng Yu-lan that was beamed on 16 February 1973 to his "old friends on Taiwan" by the People's Liberation Army's (PLA) Fukien front radio on the occasion of the Chinese New Year. Feng seemed particularly well chosen not only because he commanded respect for his scholarly achievements but also because he had been criticized in the past for being too independent of the communist line. His avowals that he had prospered in the PRC thus represented a rebuttal of the Republic of China's (ROC) claim of being the major custodian of classical Chinese culture against communist depredations.

In his talk Feng played upon Peking's international advances in the past year, pointing out that President Nixon and Prime Minister Tanaka of Japan had visited Peking and had "formally recognized that Taiwan is an inalienable part of China." In a pitch to Chinese patriotism, Feng expressed confidence that his friends "as Chinese" welcomed Peking's rising stature, and he disclosed that even prominent non-communist scholar Liang Shu-ming had been "overjoyed" at the news of the PRC's seating at the United Nations in 1971.

Aiming at the sensibilities of Taiwan intellectuals, Feng

recited a poem he had written in 1970 after receiving a personal message of regards from Mao. The poem portrayed Feng's position as an aged noncommunist intellectual who had found a home under communist rule. Even a "rotten stump of a tree" like Feng—and, by implication, intellectuals on Taiwan—was capable of "putting forth green leaves" in China under the aegis of Mao and the Chinese Communist Party (CCP).

PRC broadcasts also contained tailored appeals to ROC military officials. As a notable example, Chen Chi-hsien, the former chief of staff of the Nationalist armies in the later stages of the war against Japan and one who enjoyed a rare reputation at that time for competence and honesty, appealed to his old friends on Taiwan in a broadcast on 7 February 1973 to come to the mainland to see the many changes that had taken place. The Taiwan question figured in the 25 February 1973 memorial ceremony in Peking of another former Nationalist commander, Tseng Tse-sheng, who defected to the communists in October 1948. Speaking at the ceremony, a PRC vice defense minister declared that the grief over his death must be translated into strength in the interest of "the liberation of Taiwan." NCNA's account of the event noted that during his illness Tseng had "repeatedly expressed his hope that Taiwan would be liberated at an early date so as to realize the reunification of the motherland."

A 2 February 1973 NCNA report on Taiwan pegged to the Chinese New Year claimed that "many compatriots" there listened to the broadcasts from the mainland in order to learn about "the ever-growing new changes" in the socialist motherland. "Some were particularly moved," according to NCNA, "when they heard their relatives and friends on the air." NCNA also made a point of noting that there had been a keen demand in Taiwan for Hong Kong newspapers during President Nixon's visit to China.

The Tenth CCP Congress, August 1973

A milestone in the development of Peking's pragmatic approach in foreign affairs was reached at the Tenth CCP Congress in August 1973. In his 24 August report to the congress, Chou En-lai showed increased confidence over China's strategic position, portraying the Soviet danger as now focused against the West in Europe rather than against China. Chou offered a lengthy rationale for China's rapprochement with the United States and its continued opposition to the Soviet Union, and he implied that Peking was now secure in international affairs and would focus its attention and resources on dealing with internal questions.

Chou's treatment of foreign affairs reflected the transformed triangular relationship and Peking's trend in recent years toward pragmatic, geopolitical, and diplomatic approaches to foreign policy. Chou's report to the congress pressed the familiar line of forming "the broadest united front" against the "hegemonism of the two superpowers," but it did so in a way that clearly sanctioned the moves toward Sino-U.S. détente in the interest of counterbalancing Soviet influence. Chou's report also served as an authoritative rebuttal of a recent Soviet polemical offensive against Peking. Observing that "the Brezhnev renegade clique" had recently "talked a lot of nonsense" about Sino-Soviet relations, Chou retorted that Moscow had been playing up to monopoly capitalists by accusing Peking of opposing détente and refusing to improve Sino-Soviet relations.

Chou notably sharpened the formula of great-power rivalry that had served as the major premise of Peking's foreign policy in recent years. While noting that the superpowers "contend as well as collude" with each other, Chou advanced a clear-cut formulation of where the balance lies:

"Their collusion serves the purpose of more intensified contention. Contention is absolute and protracted, whereas collusion is relative and temporary." In the context of analyzing superpower contention, Chou cited Europe as "strategically the key point" in their rivalry. According to Chou's analysis, the West always seeks to divert the Soviet "peril" toward China, and the Soviets for their part were now feinting to the East while thrusting towards the West.

Consistent with the emphasis on pragmatic geopolitical considerations, Chou all but ignored revolutionary movements and armed struggles. In contrast, Lin Piao's ninth congress report in April 1969 had given pride of place to this subject in its discussion of foreign affairs. Typifying Peking's current approach, Chou's report hailed the awakening of the third world as "a major event in contemporary international relations," and Chinese efforts to cultivate Western Europe and Japan were reflected in Chou's reference to resentment in these areas toward superpower dominance.

Chou's report pulled few punches in its attack on the Soviets, likening Brezhnev to Hitler and all but writing off any hope for an improvement in Sino-Soviet relations. Chou recited a familar litany of charges, accusing the Kremlin of enforcing a fascist dictatorship at home and practicing "social imperialism" across the globe. He reiterated Peking's position that the dispute over "matters of principle" should not hinder normalization of state relations on the basis of peaceful coexistence, and that the border question should be settled peacefully through negotiations "free from any threat"—a formulation reflecting Peking's consistent demand for a mutual troop withdrawal from the disputed regions along the frontier. But that he made these points merely for the record seemed indicated by his sarcastic rhetorical question: "Must China give away all the territory north of the Great Wall to the Soviet revisionists" in order to demonstrate a willingness to improve Sino-Soviet relations?

Chou made a passing reference to Soviet troops massed along the Chinese border, but the most direct portrayal of a threat to China's security came in the course of an appeal for vigilance against "any war of aggression that imperialism may launch and particularly against surprise attack on our country by Soviet revisionist social imperialism." The warning against surprise attack, which was new, also appeared in the congress communiqué. Taken as a whole, however, the congress' discussion of foreign affairs did not evoke a sense of imminent threat, and Chou's report put a gloss on Mao's 20 May 1970 dictum on the danger of a new world war by asserting that it was possible "to prevent such a war."

In contrast to its attack on Moscow, Chou's report contained a directly positive assessment of the Sino-U.S. rapprochement. In the course of listing Peking's successes in foreign affairs, Chou observed that "Sino-U.S. relations have been improved to some extent." The upturn in these relations could be measured against Lin's ninth congress report, which had called the United States "the most ferocious enemy" of the world's people and had criticized the U.S. president for playing "counterrevolutionary dual tactics."

In a notable passage, Chou's report justified Peking's moves to improve Sino-U.S. relations while denigrating Soviet-U.S. détente. Distinguishing "necessary compromises between revolutionary countries and imperialist countries" from "collusion and compromise" between Moscow and Washington, Chou cited Leninist scripture for the observation that "there are compromises and compromises." Chou drove his point home by invoking Lenin's conclusion of the Brest-Litovsk treaty and contrasted it with "the doings of Khrushchev and Brezhnev" as "betrayers of Lenin."

In another justification for Sino-U.S. détente, Chou said the United States had "openly admitted that it is increasingly on the decline" and that it "could not but pull out of Vietnam." This portrayal of receding U.S. power contrasted with Chou's catalog of the "evil and foul things" perpetrated by an expansionist Soviet Union. Chou's report also echoed Peking's conciliatory approach on the Taiwan issue during the previous year, appealing to compatriots on the mainland and in Taiwan to "strive together" to liberate Taiwan and unify the country.

PRC Leadership Disputes Complicate Foreign Policy, 1974

By the end of 1973, it was clear that Peking's pragmatic approach in foreign affairs had greatly enhanced China's international position. In the course of little more than four years, Peking had marked the following major achievements:

1. Peking had managed to use the Sino-Soviet border talks to neutralize the Soviet threat against China. And it had used its active international diplomacy to block suspected Soviet efforts to keep China isolated in Asia and elsewhere.

2. Peking had gained entry into the United Nations, normalized relations with such major capitalist powers as West Germany, Japan, and Great Britain, and reestablished its traditionally favorable position among the independent communist-ruled states of North Vietnam, North Korea, and Romania. The Chinese had also begun what promised to be a fruitful reconciliation with the United States.

3. Peking had put aside its past ideological bias against increasing trade with capitalist states and had begun to open more of its markets to the advanced technology and resources available in the West, hoping thereby to build China's strength with equipment purchased abroad.

4. Peking was pursuing programs of cultural exchange

with an increasingly large number of foreign countries, thereby greatly strengthening China's appeal international-ly.

Against the backdrop of this favorable international situation, the Peking leadership intensified efforts to build China's internal political order and to develop China eco-nomically. In late 1973, for example, Peking finally ad-dressed the issue posed by the presence of inordinately strong military leaders maintaining a controlling influence in certain civilian administrative posts in the Chinese provin-ces. This problem was a holdover from the era of Lin Piao, who had died in September 1971. Chinese civilian party leaders managed to reassert their control by carrying out a long overdue transfer of military region commanders.

The wholesale transfer of all of China's military com-manders, many of whom were also provincial party chiefs, was revealed in a 1 January 1974 NCNA report of army-people gatherings on the occasion of the new year. The moves reflected a general pattern, evident since the death of Lin, to reduce the independent power of the PLA, which grew to control China's political life during the turmoil of the Cultural Revolution. While none of the military com-manders were purged, their transfer from areas where many had years of experience and personal loyalties, effectively reduced their power.

While the party leaders were apparently united on the importance of reducing the role of the military region commanders, they were far from unified on other issues. There arose at this time numerous signs of conflicts among the party leadership—conflicts apparently prompted by the fact that Chou En-lai was in declining health while Mao was not expected to live much longer. In this context, civilian leaders in Peking began to jockey for positions of power. Moderate leaders led by the ailing Chou and his protégé,

Vice Premier Teng Hsiao-ping, relied on their control of much of the state and party bureaucracies. The leftists in the leadership had no such firm base of power; they had influence in propaganda, education, and cultural organizations, but their basic support rested on Mao's sanction for their activities.

The leftists—led by Politburo members Wang Hung-wen, Chang Chun-chiao, Chiang Ching, and Yao Wen-yuan—strove to build up their own prestige within the leadership while tearing down the prestige of the moderates. In particular, they exploited the massive Chinese political campaign in 1974 to criticize Confucius and Lin Piao as a means to indirectly attack the moderates' management of Chinese affairs. Through their use of propaganda during the campaign, the leftists continually sniped at moderate policies concerning education, the rehabilitation of veteran cadre who had been criticized during the Cultural Revolution, and China's domestic economic development. The leftist-inspired anti-Confucius campaign also had a significant impact on the conduct of Chinese foreign affairs.

1. The anti-Confucius campaign led to an outpouring of harsh Chinese criticism of foreign music, films, and other cultural works. This served to curb what had been an active Chinese interest in developing cultural exchange with foreign countries.

2. The campaign prompted criticism of Chinese trade with capitalist countries. The propaganda claimed that such trade would make China dependent on "imperialism"—a line which acted to dampen Peking interest in increasing trade with the West.

3. The campaign led to an intensification of Sino-Soviet hostility. Not only did Peking media greatly expand harsh polemics against the Soviet Union, but the Chinese—for the first time since before the Sino-Soviet border clashes of

1969—publicized the arrests of alleged Soviet "spies" in the PRC. Peking gave extensive publicity to the arrest in January 1974 of Soviet diplomats in the Chinese capital and the arrest in March of that year of a Soviet helicopter crew which had landed in Sinkiang near the Sino-Soviet border. The diplomats were promptly expelled from China, leading to a quick close of that incident. But Peking decided to detain the Soviet helicopter and its crew, resulting in an exchange of sharply worded Sino-Soviet protests which marked a downturn in the already poor Sino-Soviet relationship.

4. Chinese relations with the United States also fell prey to the anti-Confucius campaign. Peking was obviously less interested in cultural exchange and trade with the United States. Chinese media criticism of the United States also increased sharply. Peking at the same time adopted an unusually strong, militant stance on the sensitive Taiwan issue, warning in shrill language that China was prepared to launch a military strike across the Taiwan Straits.

Typical of Peking's new line on Taiwan were the speeches by PRC Overseas Chinese expert Liao Cheng-chih and former Kuomintang General Fu Tso-i that marked the twenty-seventh anniversary of the 28 February 1947 Taiwan uprising against Chiang Kai-shek. The speeches shifted noticeably from the previous year's theme—that Sino-U.S. reconciliation and growing PRC international stature would eventually compel Taiwan to open negotiations with Peking—and instead stressed that Taiwan's reunion with the mainland would result from China's determination and PLA preparedness.

The PLA's role, which had been ignored in 1973, was underlined by the presence at the 1974 meeting of a high-level officer, Deputy Chief of Staff Li Ta. In noting the army's readiness to liberate Taiwan, Fu Tso-i stressed that Peking reserved the right to choose the "means by which we liberate Taiwan," and referred indirectly to U.S. naval withdrawal in raising "a cry of warning" to Taipei that "the Taiwan Straits are today no longer an obstacle to the liberation of Taiwan."

Neither Chinese spokesman indicated any specific plan for PLA action concerning Taiwan, stressing the army's general defensive "vigilance" and "readiness." By using such evidence of Chinese resolve, they strove to admonish officials and people on Taiwan not to miss the present "opportunity" to promote "peaceful liberation" of the island. Both duly reiterated past themes of reconciliation and patriotic unity in calling for continued Taiwanese visits to the mainland and in advising that whether they come forward early or late, "all patriots belong to one big family." They also appeared to reflect a stiffening in Peking's attitude toward the top members of the Chiang government, in contrast to the previous year when Peking pointedly sanctioned reconciliation with Chiang by noting the precedent of Mao's talks with Chiang in Chungking in 1945. In 1974 Liao Cheng-chih referred harshly to the "Chiang family dynasty" and acknowledged that in Taipei "a few are traitors" who will not work for reunification.

Peking's harder line was also directed against alleged foreign intervention on the island, particularly by the USSR and Japanese right-wing groups. By contrast, the Chinese in 1973 had confidently endeavored to show that the Sino-U.S. agreement in the Shanghai communiqué implied that Washington would not allow another foreign force to interfere on the island. This time Liao Cheng-chih warned Taipei against attempting to "flirt" with Moscow and indirectly denounced Japanese rightists in noting that "a handful of diehards abroad" are "still vainly attempting to dip their fingers into the pie of Taiwan."

Fourth National People's Congress, January 1975

Chou En-lai and the moderates in the Chinese leadership managed to weather the impact of the leftist challenge during the anti-Confucius campaign. Foreign policy resumed a generally pragmatic approach by the end of 1974, and Chou took the opportunity of his 13 January 1975 report to the Fourth National People's Congress (NPC) to reaffirm Peking's commitment to a pragmatic, geopolitical approach to foreign affairs. However, the PRC leadership disputes over power in China remained unresolved. Thus, for example, leftist standard bearer Chang Chun-chiao was appointed vice premier at the NPC and began taking a more active role in the management of Chinese foreign policy. At the same time, Chou's protégé Teng Hsiao-ping received a boost in his career as a result of the 8-10 January 1975 CCP plenum which had preceded the NPC, where he had been designated party vice chairman.

In dealing with foreign affairs in his report to the NPC, Chou generally maintained the views he had presented in his report at the tenth party congress in August 1973—his last comprehensive discussion of foreign affairs. His much briefer NPC report was particularly notable for its image of a world situation markedly favorable to China. Chou did give more credence to the possibility that contention between the superpowers could lead to world war, but his remarks were couched in a theoretical framework and did not picture China as threatened. He assessed Sino-U.S. relations in positive terms, but he bluntly characterized Sino-Soviet relations as at a standstill.

Chou departed somewhat from the PRC line on world war and revolution that had been standard for almost five years. He said that the "fierce contention" between the United States and the Soviet Union "is bound to lead to world war some day," and he was equivocal as to whether war or revolution was more likely, saying that "the factors for both war and revolution are increasing." By contrast, Chou at the tenth party congress had quoted the passage in Mao Tse-tung's 20 May 1970 statement: that while "the danger of the new world war still exists," revolution against imperialism is the "main trend" in the world today. The Mao formulation had been frequently quoted in authoritative Chinese comment up to that time. Reflecting his balanced view of war and revolution, Chou appeared sanguine about the strength of the third world, and he declared that "whether war gives rise to revolution or revolution prevents war, in either case the international situation will develop in a direction favorable to the people. . . ." This assertion was similar to Lin Piao's remark at the Ninth CCP Congress in April 1969 when he had cited a quotation from Mao to the effect that either world war would give rise to revolution or revolution would prevent war.

Chou's remark on the inevitability at some future time of a military confrontation between the two superpowers seemed aimed primarily at disparaging the notion of a possible relaxation of U.S.-Soviet tensions under the cover of détente. Referring to recent talk of détente and peace around the world, Chou maintained that all the talk merely proves that "there is no détente, let alone lasting peace, in this world." Assessing what he saw as progressively increasing U.S.-Soviet contention for world control, Chou indicated that the developing "economic crisis in the capitalist world" at that time had served to intensify U.S.-Soviet competition, and he repeated his judgment at the tenth party congress that Europe was the focus of U.S.-Soviet rivalry.

Chou was more sanguine about China's own national security than he had been in 1973. He repeated his 1973 slogan playing down the Soviet Union's threat to China in noting that Moscow merely "makes a feint to the east while attacking in the west," and he dropped his 1973 additional allegation that the West had always sought to divert the Soviet threat eastward, toward China. Chou also dropped his 1973 admonition against the possible launching of an imperialist war against China and his special warning against "surprise attack" from the USSR. His routine instructions on national defense included calls for the people to maintain "vigilance" and to be "prepared" against war. (In 1973 Chou had enjoined the people to maintain *"high* vigilance" and to be *"fully* prepared" against war.)

Chou voiced continued support for Peking's flexible foreign policy approach under the banner of Mao's "revolutionary line in foreign affairs," and he gave highlighted attention to improving ties with the developed countries of the so-called second world. Thus, he offered Peking's highest level endorsement for Western European unity against superpower threats and bullying, and voiced Chinese readiness to promote friendly relations with Japan on the basis of the 1972 Sino-Japanese statements. Chou routinely reaffirmed China's intention never to be a superpower, its solidarity with the third world, and its intention to uphold proletarian internationalism. He also promised to enhance ties with "socialist countries."

Chou echoed his assessment at the tenth party congress that Sino-U.S. relations "have improved to some extent." However, he added a phrase giving credit to the United States as well as to the PRC, stating that improvement had been achieved through "joint efforts of both sides." Though Chou noted that "there exist fundamental differences between China and the United States," he expressed confidence that bilateral relations would continue to improve so long as the two countries carry out "in earnest" the principles of the Shanghai communiqué.

Chou's assurance stood in contrast to his defensive 1973

assessment of PRC ties with Washington, when he had gone to great lengths to rationalize the need for "necessary compromises between revolutionary countries and imperialist countries." Suggesting that at that time he was having some difficulty justifying Sino-U.S. détente to more rigid ideologues at home or abroad, Chou at the party congress had cited Leninist scripture to distinguish Peking's new policy from Soviet collaboration with Washington.

Chou did not repeat his 1973 references to U.S. "defeats" in Korea and Vietnam and to the "decline" of U.S. power over the past generation. And, although he continued to list the United States ahead of the Soviet Union in commenting on the superpowers, he dropped all reference to "U.S. imperialism," which had been cited frequently in his 1973 report. By contrast, he continued to refer to "Soviet social imperialism." The premier gave only routine attention to Taiwan, reaffirming determination to "liberate" the island while calling on "fellow countrymen" on Taiwan to join in the liberation struggle.

Though his discussion of the USSR was shorter and less polemical than his anti-Soviet diatribe at the 1973 party congress, Chou characterized Sino-Soviet relations as at a standstill, openly attacked Soviet "deception" on the border issue, and challenged Moscow to meet Chinese demands concerning the frontier. Chou accused the "Soviet leading clique" of having betrayed Marxism-Leninism and of having taken a series of actions—including subversion and provoking of armed clashes along the frontier—to worsen state relations with China. Chou repeated recent Chinese charges concerning the Sino-Soviet border and the Peking border talks which had previously been put forth in the Chinese message to the USSR on the 6 November 1974 anniversary of the October Revolution and in an article in the December 1974 issue of the Chinese journal *Historical*

Studies. Chou's charges represented the premier's first public discussion of the Sino-Soviet border talks, as well as Peking's first authoritative comment on the substance of the negotiations, since they had begun in October 1969.

Chou claimed that Moscow was totally responsible for the lack of progress because it had refused to adhere to the PRC-USSR understanding reached during the September 1969 meeting between Chou and Kosygin in Peking that had led to the start of the talks. He said that the understanding included an accord on mutual nonaggression and nonuse of force, as well as an agreement to withdraw forces from disputed border areas. Chou said that Moscow had refused to withdraw from, and had even denied the existence of, disputed border areas. He accused the Russians of talking profusely about "empty treaties" on nonuse of force and nonaggression in order to deceive Soviet and world opinion, and advised Moscow to stop its "deceitful tricks," negotiate honestly, and "do something" to solve "a bit" of the border problem. Chou's statement served notice on the Soviet Union that it must make the next move to improve relations.

Policy in East Asia, 1975

In 1975 Chinese foreign policy was dominated by Peking's concern over what it saw as a major shift in the balance of power in East Asia. Although Chinese leftist leaders continued to snipe at the implementation of moderate policies—voicing such criticism during the course of the domestic ideological campaign on the ancient Chinese novel *The Water Margin*—leftist influence on PRC foreign policy was not strong. Geopolitical concerns stemming particularly from the rapid collapse of the U.S. position in Indochina in spring 1975 prompted stepped up Chinese efforts in pragmatic, conventional diplomacy designed to stabilize the East Asian balance of power to prevent further

Soviet expansion.

The Sino-U.S. relationship had remained the centerpiece of PRC strategy in the region since the issuing of the February 1972 Shanghai communique. In accord with Peking's interests, Washington continued to implement the Nixon doctrine, gradually withdrawing from forward positions in Southeast Asia, Taiwan, and Japan. At the same time, the United States repeatedly made clear that its withdrawal should not be interpreted as a sign of U.S. weakness, and that Washington remained firmly opposed to any other power's attempts to gain a dominant position in East Asia— this applied especially to the Soviet Union. The Nixon administration kept sufficient force on hand to back up its stance, thereby reassuring Peking that the Shanghai communiqué's provisions against any one power's establishment of "hegemony" in East Asia would be fulfilled.

Events surrounding the rapid collapse of U.S.-backed regimes in Cambodia and South Vietnam in the spring of 1975 upset the steady development of an East Asian balance favorable to Chinese interests. From Peking's viewpoint, the stability of the newly emerging East Asian order had met with a significant setback. While Peking had expected the United States to withdraw eventually from Indochina, the precipitous U.S. pullback held serious implications for China's interests. The United States had suffered a serious defeat at a time when U.S. leadership and resolve abroad, particularly in East Asia, had already been called into question as a result of the Watergate affair and the 1974-75 economic recession. (Peking media had noted the debilitating impact of the economic "crisis" on U.S. internal and international strength from the very outset of the recession. The Chinese leaders were also reported by the Western press to have been seriously concerned over the fall of the Nixon administration, though Peking media discreetly remained virtually silent on the matter.)

Against this backdrop, the U.S. defeats in Indochina cast some doubt on a key premise in Peking's plan for a new East Asian order. In particular, was the United States now strong enough, and more important, was it resolute enough to continue to serve as the main strategic block against Soviet encroachment and advances in East Asia? An analysis of Chinese media behavior demonstrated that Peking judged that the United States had indeed been weakened by the Indochina events, and that U.S. strength and resolve in East Asia had been significantly affected. Shifts in Chinese media treatment reflected an altered Chinese perception of the balance of forces in the area: they saw the United States as less influential in Asia, and thus viewed Washington's utility as a bulwark against future Soviet expansion as somewhat compromised.

The Chinese responded to their perception of an altered East Asian situation in several ways.

1. Peking demonstrated that it continued to adhere to the Sino-U.S. plan for a new East Asian order as articulated in the antihegemony clause of the Shanghai communiqué. But, whereas in the past Peking had relied mainly on U.S. strength to sustain the favorable balance, the Chinese began to take on a greater responsibility in their own right for shoring up East Asian positions against Soviet expansion. In particular, Peking moved adroitly to solidify China's relations with, and to cement anti-Soviet feelings in, the two noncommunist states in East Asia most affected by the collapse of the U.S. position in Indochina—the Philippines and Thailand. Peking's establishment of diplomatic relations with these states—employing in each instance a joint communiqué testifying to both sides' opposition to international "hegemony"—was intended to reassure Manila and Bangkok of their security and stability in the wake of the

U.S. defeat. In particular, China's reassurances to both governments had precluded the possibility that Manila and Bangkok, in a hasty search for big power support in the new Southeast Asian situation, might have moved into a one-sided relationship with the USSR. (China of course had long wished to normalize relations with these states, if possible on the basis of principles inimical to the USSR. But the speed with which Peking exploited these governments' new interest in relations with China after the Indochina events, and the unusually blunt Chinese stress on anti-Soviet invective during negotiations, showed heightened PRC concern to offset what was seen as growing possibilities for Soviet expansion in the face of the U.S. withdrawal.)

2. Peking acknowledged that the United States had been "beaten black and blue" in Indochina, and noted that the Asian people, especially those in Southeast Asia, were increasingly successful in efforts to drive the "wolf"—the United States—from the "front gate." But the Chinese made plain that they were opposed to any unilateral, rapid U.S. withdrawal from international involvement as a result of this setback. They clearly indicated that they wished the United States to remain heavily involved abroad, and strategically vigilant against the USSR in Europe, the Middle East, and Asia. Peking went so far as to stress a propaganda line that the U.S. defeats in Indochina had actually presented the United States with an "opportunity" to pull back from "secondary" areas where it had been overextended, in order too serve more effectively as a strategic bulwark against Soviet expansion into more "vital" areas abroad. In this vein, Peking reduced past criticism of U.S. military presence and political influence in Asia, and gave unusually favorable play to U.S. statements of resolve to retain strong ties with Japan and selected noncommunist Asian states, and to maintain a strong naval presence in the western Pacific and

the Indian Ocean.

3. Peking viewed the USSR as a more immediate and serious threat to China's aspirations in East and Southeast Asia than it had in the early seventies. Accordingly, the Chinese adopted a more active policy against the USSR, focused on blocking Moscow's attempts to advance along China's flanks as the United States withdrew. In particular, the Chinese launched a major propaganda campaign to warn Asian states of the danger posed by the ravenous "tiger"—the USSR—lurking at the rear door as the Asians pushed the "wolf" through the front gate. Peking also laid special stress on criticizing Moscow's plan for a collective security system in Asia as a thinly veiled Soviet effort to achieve political "hegemony" in Asia, portraying it as the direct antithesis of the "antihegemony front" fostered by China and its friends. Peking's higher profile against the USSR caused the Chinese to view with increased suspicion Asian states which maintained cordial relations with Moscow, notably communist Vietnam.

Peking had stepped up propaganda efforts to encourage the United States to remain actively involved against the USSR in Asia and elsewhere abroad even before the final collapse of the pro-U.S. regimes in Cambodia and South Vietnam. The Chinese notably began playing up favorably statements by U.S. officials indicating continued U.S. resolve abroad despite its setbacks in Indochina. Peking media pointedly disparaged third party speculation that portrayed the U.S. defeats as an indication of a decline of U.S. will to defend its allies and prime interests abroad.

The Chinese at the same time began a strident propaganda effort designed to point out the dangers of Soviet intentions in Asian areas where in the past the United States had been portrayed as the main enemy. For example, criticism of Soviet actions in Indochina soon even surpassed the criticism of U.S. actions in the area, as Chinese comment focused the brunt of its invective against the USSR.

Two NCNA reports of 13 April 1975, responding to President Ford's 10 April foreign policy address to Congress, only mildly censured the president's request for last minute aid to stave off the collapse of the Thieu government. Rather, the reports focused on the thesis that the setbacks in Indochina had provided an opportunity for Washington to cut its losses in such secondary areas and to concentrate on checking Soviet advances in more strategically important areas, such as Europe, the Middle East, and Japan. NCNA also confirmed Peking's desire to keep the Sino-U.S. relationship on course by citing the president's remarks on developing U.S. ties with Peking, including his prediction that relations would be enhanced during his visit to the PRC later in 1975.

The first NCNA report on the president's address balanced criticism of continued U.S. intervention in Vietnam with implicit Chinese satisfaction conveyed in its detailing of the president's remarks suggesting continued U.S. vigilance against the Soviet Union. NCNA noted that the president's address showed that the United States "has no intention of discontinuing its interventionist policy toward South Vietnam" and that he was requesting emergency aid for Saigon, "more than double" his earlier requests, on the "pretext" that the United States "could not abandon [its] friends." NCNA then focused on the president's remarks on the U.S.-Soviet relationship, noting his characterization of current Moscow-Washington ties as "still a competitive relationship" as well as his declaration that "as long as I am President, we will not permit détente to become a license to fish in troubled waters."

Peking's mild criticism of the president's new Vietnam aid request was softened further by the second NCNA report, which played up U.S. press reports that U.S. officials were resigned to Saigon's collapse and now were moving to revitalize U.S. foreign policy by withdrawing from "overextended" positions in Asia and focusing on areas more vital to U.S. interests. The report pointed up Peking's interest in seeing the United States pitted against the Soviet Union in other areas after the U.S. pullback from Southeast Asia. It publicized the view expressed in the U.S. press that recent events in Vietnam and Cambodia had forced the United States to concentrate on "what's really important." In this context, NCNA called favorable attention to President Ford's reaffirmation of close ties with Japan, and replayed press reports that leaders in Tokyo were pleased with the thrust of U.S. policy as Washington withdrew from Indochina.

Peking's exuberant welcome for the communist victories in Cambodia and South Vietnam contrasted with past comment on these areas by including especially harsh invective against the USSR, while treating the United States with restraint. The 30 April NCNA report on the U.S. evacuation of Saigon even played up favorably comment by President Ford and Secretary Kissinger calling for a new U.S. consensus on foreign policy that would allow the United States to select carefully and firmly maintain commitments abroad, and in particular to forge a new policy in East Asia better suited to present circumstances. On the other hand, Chinese comment stressed warnings against the superpower "which carries the signboard of socialism" and "burns with ambition" to engage in "frantic expansion."

The Chinese response to the forceful U.S. military action to secure the release of the ship *Mayaguez,* captured by Cambodian forces in May, also treated the United States with restraint while taking great pains to criticize the USSR over the incident. A 21 May NCNA correspondent's report tempered Peking's anti-U.S. criticism by presenting the U.S.

military action against Cambodia as an aberration caused by "political need" to shore up the U.S. international position after the Indochina defeat. NCNA claimed that the United States had used the *Mayaguez* affair as a "typical farce of self-consolation" in reaction to its failure in Indochina. This article stated that instead of boosting morale and improving its international image, the United States had further damaged both, asserting more bluntly than usual that the *Mayaguez* incident had "given the paper tiger more signs of wear and tear."

The NCNA critique discreetly did not refer to the Ford administration explicitly and balanced its anti-U.S. flavor with sharp jabs at the USSR, devoting its middle paragraph to attacking "apologists from Moscow" allegedly trying to "whitewash" the U.S. actions.

A more vivid reflection of the altered PRC view of the superpowers in Asia was seen in Peking's use of the fifth anniversary of Mao's 20 May 1970 statement—the major Chinese anti-U.S. polemic that had been prompted by the U.S. military incursion into Cambodia—to attack sharply the Soviet Union's policy in Indochina. The Chinese employed only routine criticism of the United States. The anniversary was marked by a *People's Daily* editorial plus a Peking-radio signed commentary, unlike the previous three anniversaries, which saw only a signed article in *People's Daily*. Those previous anniversary commentaries had progressively deemphasized the Indochina slant of Mao's statement, focusing instead on denunciations of U.S.-Soviet efforts to reach international détente. The current revived stress on Indochina accorded with Peking's efforts since the Cambodian and Vietnamese successes in April to play up the Indochinese victories as proof of the "correctness" of Mao's judgment—expressed in the May 1970 statement—that a small nation can defeat a powerful aggressor.

The Chinese comment did list the United States ahead of the USSR in referring critically to the two superpowers' policies, but Peking's harsher criticism of the Soviet Union this time was a striking departure from the spirit of the originally strong anti-U.S. statement. The editorial routinely criticized the U.S. "aggressors" for extending the Indochina war in 1970, but charged that Moscow had openly sided with Lon Nol and had also done "its utmost to undermine the antiimperialist revolutionary struggle of the Indochinese people." The Peking radio commentary also played up the "ugly performance" of the USSR in Cambodia, charging among other things that Moscow had shot an "arrow at the victorious Cambodian people from behind" by its labeling of the communists' struggle there as a "fratricidal war" instead of a war of national liberation.

A 16 June Peking radio program offered the most comprehensive assessment of the altered situation in Southeast Asia in the months following the U.S. Indochina defeats. Unlike earlier Chinese coverage, consisting mainly of replays of third party comment, the article offered an assessment in Peking's own name; this program was not beamed abroad, but was designed chiefly to explain Peking's current views on the superpowers to the internal Chinese audience.

The article acknowledged that the United States had become "increasingly weak and strategically passive" in Southeast Asia in the wake of its Indochina defeat. The commentary reported that Washington had been forced to withdraw somewhat and to "readjust its strategic deployment," but also noted approvingly that the United States "is reluctant to abandon its interests in the region" to alleged encroachment by the USSR. It acknowledged for the first time Assistant Secretary of State Habib's spring tour of Southeast Asia following Saigon's fall, viewing the trip as evidence of U.S. determination to maintain a position as an

"Asian and Pacific country" and to play "its deserved and responsible role for the sake of the interests of the United States and this region."

By contrast, the Soviet Union was treated with extreme prejudice. Moscow was bluntly assailed as the main threat to Southeast Asian stability and as an ambitious, aggressive superpower trying hard "to replace the United States and dominate Asia."

Peking's analysis was supported by other coverage giving unusually full NCNA reportage to favorable U.S. comment on the U.S. Navy's Indian Ocean presence and planned base at Diego Garcia. Peking also favorably reported the New Zealand prime minister's recent ringing endorsement of the ANZUS pact with the United States, and maintained silence on other security pacts in the area. By contrast, Soviet diplomatic, military, economic, and espionage efforts throughout the Western Pacific and in East Asia were repeatedly criticized, with NCNA viewing Moscow's proposal for a "collective security system" in Asia as an ill-disguised attempt to dominate East Asia just as the Japanese militarists had done during World War II.

Relations with Japan

Peking's altered perception of the superpowers, and of the general strategic balance in East Asia, also had a marked impact on China's approach toward important East Asian states. In the case of Japan, for example, Chinese media coverage encouraged closer U.S.-Japan strategic ties to defend against what was seen as an increasingly menacing Soviet threat. Chinese media virtually dropped past criticism of U.S.-Japan ties while notably increasing their attacks against Soviet intentions. Thus, NCNA reported the 5-6 August talks between President Ford and Prime Minister Miki without the usual reproaches on U.S.-Japan defense

ties. At the same time, Chinese reports on 14 August sharply
criticized Soviet pressure on Japan, in contrast to the anti-
U.S. invective that had been issued in the past on that date—
the anniversary of V-J Day.

A 7 August NCNA report highlighted passages from the
U.S.-Japan joint announcement following Ford's talks with
Miki which emphasized the importance both sides attached
to the U.S.-Japan security treaty, and noted that "the continued maintenance of the treaty serves the long-term interests of both countries." NCNA replayed the announcement's
affirmation that the United States would continue to abide
by its defense commitment to Japan, and cited without
adverse comment President Ford's statement that the United
States "would continue to play an active and positive role in
that region and would continue to uphold its commitments
there." By contrast, Peking's coverage of the last official visit
by a Japanese prime minister to the United States—a 3
August 1973 report on former prime minister Tanaka's talks
with then president Nixon—had ignored both sides' stress in
their joint communiqué on the importance of the U.S.-
Japan security treaty.

In reporting that the two leaders had discussed "a wide
range" of economic problems, NCNA avoided references to
U.S.-Japanese friction over trade and financial matters that
in the past had been a staple of Chinese comment. Peking
even noted with apparent approval that both leaders had
"welcomed" a dialogue between oil producers and consum-
ers. The 3 August 1973 NCNA report on talks with former
prime minister Tanaka had cited alleged "contradictions"
between the two leaders on trade and fiscal policies, noting
news reports that Tanaka felt that the United States and
Japan were both "partners and competitors."

On 14 August the Chinese media, as usual, did not
explicitly acknowledge the thirtieth anniversary of the defeat

of Japan in the Pacific war, but used the date to issue two sharply worded reports attacking Soviet military threats and pressure against Japan. On the last quinquennial of that date in 1970, Peking similarly had avoided explicit acknowledgment of V-J Day but had issued a lengthy NCNA attack on the United States for its alleged military occupation and pressure on Japan.

The current NCNA reports underlined wide-ranging Chinese criticisms of Soviet policy toward Japan, claiming that Moscow was employing "tough and soft tactics of military threat and economic lure" to bring Japan into its sphere of influence. One report broke new ground regarding both tactics by depicting Soviet military bases on the Japanese-claimed "northern territories" as "a dagger directed against Japan" and by pointing to a "new trick" regarding alleged efforts by Moscow to get the Japanese involved in a so-called "new plan for developing Siberia" following its failure to get them involved in exploitation of the Tyumen oil field in Siberia. The report stressed the Soviet military threat to Japan, stating that Moscow only needed to move its forces "slightly" in order to land troops on the main northern Japanese island of Hokkaido, "as the troops of the old tsar did in the past." It added Japanese press comment that Japan's air space from "Hokkaido to Okinawa" and the "whole of Japan" had been "put under the shadows of Soviet naval and air force might."

Though the articles duly portrayed Moscow's efforts as fundamentally designed to contend with the United States for hegemony in Asia, NCNA carefully avoided all reference to the U.S. bases or military presence in Japan. It even went to some pains to depict the United States and Japan as mutually threatened by Soviet expansion. For instance, one report said that Soviet naval maneuvers around Japan "pose a threat to the U.S. Pacific fleet and directly to Japan's security" and also stated that Soviet bases in the northern territories were targeted for use against the United States as well as Japan.

Relations with Southeast Asia

Toward the noncommunist states in Southeast Asia, which had heretofore relied on the U.S. presence in the area as a major source of regional stability, the Chinese adopted a somewhat different posture. The Chinese media notably avoided stress on the need for continued reliance on U.S. military forces or political influence. Rather, they placed extraordinary emphasis on the importance of closer relations with China, under conditions inimical to the USSR, as a source of stability in the area. At the same time, regional self-reliance and cooperation, especially under the auspices of such organizations as the Association of Southeast Asian States (ASEAN), was deemed as having a stabilizing effect, contrary to Moscow's interests. Predictably, the USSR was characterized as the main and growing danger to the region, while past Chinese criticism of the United States was muffled.

Typical of China's new approach was the comment during the visits to China of President Marcos of the Philippines and Prime Minister Khukrit of Thailand in June 1975. Vice Premier Teng Hsiao-ping, speaking to Khukrit at a Peking banquet on 30 June, focused exclusively on the USSR as the present strategic danger to Southeast. Speaking in the usual euphemisms, Teng said that while one of the "superpowers" had suffered defeat and had to withdraw from Indochina,

> the other superpower with wild ambitions has extended its tentacles far and wide. It insatiably seeks new military bases in Southeast Asia and sends its naval vessels

to ply the Indian and West Pacific Oceans, posing a menacing threat to the peace and security of the Southeast Asian countries. The spectre of its expansionism now haunts Southeast Asia, as it hankers for converting this region into its sphere of influence some day.

Followup comment on the Thai prime minister's visit went to unusual lengths to stress the importance of China's new relations with Southeast Asian countries, under terms including the "antihegemony clause." It went beyond earlier reports in Peking media which had said merely that the establishment of relations between the PRC and Southeast Asian countries would strengthen the unity and cooperation of the third world. Peking's current reportage was unusually explicit in portraying Chinese efforts to include "antihegemony" clauses in recent communiqués with states throughout the Asia-Pacific region as an effective means of countering Soviet ambitions to dominate the area under the cover of a Soviet-fostered "Asian collective security system."

NCNA reports of Thai comment focused on the antihegemony clause as "the most important thing" contained in the 1 July Sino-Thai joint communiqué, on 4 July quoting a Thai editorial applauding the Sino-Thai statement as having "further strengthened. . .the antihegemony front." After duly warning against "intensified Soviet expansion in Southeast Asia," NCNA cited the Thai editorial's observation that the "surest guarantee for security and peace in Southeast Asia" is to "reinforce the antihegemony movement" in the area.

Peking reports of Thai comment on 9 and 10 July depicted the Sino-Thai communiqué, as well as Peking's proposed inclusion of the antihegemony clause in its planned peace treaty with Japan, as an effective rebuff of Soviet attempts to meddle in Asian affairs and use the Asian collective security proposal to dominate the continent. The articles warned that Asians must be more wary of Soviet intentions in the wake of the U.S. pullback from the area, and they portrayed Peking's establishment of relations with Thailand as "beneficial to the security and peace in the region" because this had caused the USSR, "seeking hegemony everywhere," to become "greatly panic stricken."

The changes in China's perception of the U.S.-Soviet balance in East Asia, and Peking's resulting greater concern over Soviet penetration along China's southern and eastern frontiers, resulted in a serious downturn in China's heretofore cordial relations with communist Vietnam. The Chinese showed undisguised apprehension that the Vietnamese communists, now free from the U.S. threat and less solicitous of China's view, might choose to pursue policies less agreeable with PRC interests in Southeast Asia. Peking was especially concerned that Hanoi might develop closer ties with the USSR in the postwar situation, using relations with Moscow as a source of leverage to block the expansion of Chinese influence in Southeast Asia as the United States withdrew.

Peking's strategy to counter suspected Soviet encroachments in Indochina was similar to its strategy in Southeast Asia as a whole. The Chinese encouraged Indochinese states to be self-reliant and to establish closer relations with China in order to block the intervention of both "superpowers" in the area. The results of China's efforts were less successful than they had been in noncommunist Southeast Asian states. The new Cambodian government, which had never received significant support from the USSR during its war against Lon Nol, was willing to go along with Peking. Deputy Prime Minister Khieu Samphan of Cambodia, during an August 1975 visit to China, signed a joint communiqué with Chinese leaders in which both sides condemned the international policies of both "superpowers" and in which China was singled out for praise as a "steel bulwark" of the world "socialist movement."

By contrast, Hanoi's leadership continued to cultivate close relations with the USSR. Peking demonstrated its dissatisfaction by publicly stressing before Vietnamese audiences—for the first time in years—sensitive issues of the Sino-Soviet polemic, and by withholding past routine expressions of Sino-Vietnamese solidarity. Such Chinese behavior was seen most vividly in Chinese commemoration of the DRV's thirtieth anniversary celebrations and in Peking's treatment of a visiting top level Vietnamese delegation later that month.

Celebrations in Peking in early september 1975 marking the thirtieth DRV National Day were at a lower level than Chinese commemorations of the DRV's quinquennial anniversaries of 1965 and 1970, and the Chinese expressions of friendship and solidarity were also more reserved than in the past. Peking's treatment of the anniversary included the customary congratulatory message from Mao Tse-tung, Chu Te, and Chou En-lai on 1 September and a *People's Daily* editorial on 2 September. There was also the usual 2 September DRV envoy's reception in Peking, attended that year by CCP Politburo members Teng Hsiao-ping, Yao Wen-yuan, and Wu Te (the latter addressed the gathering).

Peking celebrations for the last decennial anniversary, the twentieth in 1965, had been considerably higher in level. The DRV envoy's reception in Peking that year had occasioned a heavier PRC leadership turnout, including six Politburo members, and had been addressed by Chou En-lai. Peking had also held a large rally attended by five Politburo members and addressed by Peking Mayor Peng Chen. Similarly, the less important twenty-fifth anniversary in 1970 had occasioned a slightly higher level treatment in Peking than was the case in 1975: there had been a rally, attended by three CCP Politburo members and addressed by Vice Premier Li Hsien-nien, and the DRV envoy's reception drew three Politburo members and had been again addressed by Chou En-lai.

Peking's expressions of Sino-Vietnamese solidarity and support were even more reserved in comparison with those employed in marking the DRV's twenty-ninth anniversary in 1974. In the leaders' message in 1974, Mao, Chu, and Chou had expressed their "warmest greetings," while this time they extended "warm congratulations." Their 1975 message hailed the "militant unity and revolutionary friendship" between the two peoples; the message in 1974 had praised their "deep revolutionary friendship and militant solidarity based on Marxism-Leninism principles and proletarian internationalism" and had included a pledge to continue to perform "international duties" of supporting the Vietnamese people's "just cause." The 2 September *People's Daily* editorial in 1974 had included in full long-standard expressions of Sino-Vietnamese solidarity, as "nourished personally by Chairman Mao and President Ho on the basis of Marxism-Leninism and proletarian internationalism," and had reiterated the leaders' message pledge to perform "proletarian internationalist duties." By contrast, the editorial this time characterized the two countries as "friendly socialist neighbors" and "close comrades-in-arms," and only expressed hope that the "militant friendship" between them would be continuously consolidated and developed.

Marking the anniversary in a 3 September 1975 speech at a steel mill in Vietnam, Vice Premier Chen Hsi-lien of the PRC took the occasion to polemically admonish the Vietnamese on the sensitive issue of the danger in Southeast Asia and the world of the intensified competition of "both" superpowers. Chen assured his Vietnamese audience that the consolidation of the "fraternal friendship and militant solidarity" between the two nations on the basis of Marxism-Leninism and proletarian internationalism conformed to the "fundamental interests" and constituted the "common desire" of the two peoples. He also recalled that in the past struggle against "U.S. imperialist aggression," the Chinese had supported Vietnam "to the best of our ability" as "an international obligation incumbent upon us," and he affirmed that China would do its "utmost" to consolidate relations in the future. At the same time, the vice premier said that "we must take notice" of superpower rivalry as "the root cause" of world unrest and the source of "a new world war." While noting that superpower contention was focused in the West, Chen affirmed that the superpowers were "doing their utmost to place other countries under their sphere of influence" in Asia as well, and he added specific praise for Southeast Asian countries' continuing struggle against "superpower intervention."

Chinese handling of the 22-28 September 1975 visit to Peking by a Vietnamese party-government delegation led by First Secretary Le Duan of the Vietnamese Worker's Party (VWP) was noticeably less effusive than it had been for Le Duan's last visit as head of an official delegation in June 1973. Peking comment moderated previous expressions of unity and friendship and gave more attention to assessments (potentially offensive to Vietnamese sensitivities) of the world situation and of the superpowers than it had during the 1973 stay.

Expressions of Sino-Vietnamese friendship and solidarity in Vice Premier Teng Hsaio-ping's 22 September banquet speech for the DRV guests were less elaborate than those in the speech by Premier Chou En-lai welcoming Le Duan in 1973. While Chou had characterized the two nations as "close comrades-in-arms and brothers" who "shared weal and woe" and had gone through "thick and thin" together, Teng now called the PRC and Vietnam "fraternal socialist neighbors" sharing a "longstanding traditional friendship." In his speech Chou had noted that a "profound revolutionary friendship, nurtured personally by Mao Tse-tung and Ho Chi Minh and based on the principles of Marxism-Leninism and proletarian internationalism," had been forged between the two nations and that the "great friendship and militant unity" between them had been "further enhanced and consolidated." Chou had pledged that China would continue to perform its internationalist duty to resolutely support Vietnam's "just struggle." This time Teng merely noted that the Chinese people have "always treasured their revolutionary friendship" with Vietnam, that the preservation and development of their friendship on the basis of Marxism-Leninism and proletarian internationalism was in keeping with the "common desire" and "fundamental interests" of the two peoples, and that the Chinese people would "spare no effort" to do so.

The *People's Daily* editorial greeting Le Duan's arrival in 1975 similarly dropped most of the expressions of friendship that had been recited in the editorial greeting his 1973 visit. It pledged only that the Chinese "will, as always, actively contribute their share" to strengthening Sino-Vietnamese friendship. Atmospherics in the NCNA reports on the delegation's arrival and its reception by the Chinese leadership were also moderated. While the Sino-Vietnamese talks in 1973 had been opened in a "warm atmosphere overflowing with revolutionary friendship and militant unity," talks this time were characterized simply as "fraternal, cordial, and friendly."

Similiar to Chen Hsi-lien's emphasis on 3 September, Teng's speech on the 22nd stressed, without specifically mentioning the United States and the Soviet Union, that the hegemonism of the "superpowers" was the primary cause of world tension today. He warned his Vietnamese listeners that the superpowers were subjecting the third world to "aggression , subversion, interference, control, and plunder," and pledged that China would "stand unswervingly" at the side of the third world countries as the "main force" of resistance to imperialism, colonialism, and hegemonism. During Le Duan's 1973 visit, by contrast, Chou En-lai did not comment on the world situation, discussing only the "completely new situation" in Indochina in the wake of the Paris peace agreements.

Campaign against U.S.-Soviet Détente, 1975-1976

By late 1975, Peking began to see the situation in East Asia in a more optimistic light. Even though U.S. power and influence in the region had been weakened, the United States continued to demonstrate an active interest and involvement in maintaining an East Asian balance of power that would preclude heavy Soviet penetration into the region. This was underlined by President Ford in late 1975 when he announced the so-called Pacific Doctrine. This strategic policy in East Asia following defeat in Indochina was based on U.S. air and naval power in the region, and on close U.S. ties with its traditional allies, such as Japan, and with the PRC. It significantly avoided mentioning any major role that the Soviet Union might play in the area.

Meanwhile, Peking had achieved considerable success over the past few months in broadening its influence among noncommunist Southeast Asian states. The Chinese propaganda line warning against the danger of Soviet expansion as the United States withdrew also was winning new adherents in Southeast Asia. At the end of 1975, the only areas in East Asia where the Soviet Union maintained considerable influence were Vietnam and Laos.

Peking still could not afford to be overly optimistic about the broad international trend of East-West relations, however. While feeling more secure in East Asia, the Chinese showed new alarm over signs in late 1975 concerning what they saw as a less resolute Western posture vis-à-vis the Soviet Union. In particular, the August 1975 East-West summit meeting in Helsinki of the European Security Conference was viewed by Peking as evidence of a growing trend in the United States and the West to "appease" the Soviet Union in order to direct the Soviet menace "eastward," away from Europe. Peking responded with warnings to the West against "appeasement" of Soviet "expansionism" under the cover of détente. It stepped up propaganda concerning the danger of a new world war that, it charged, would be started by the Soviet Union. It also became more critical of what it viewed as Western attempts to capitulate before the USSR.

Typical of Peking's stepped up antidétente rhetoric following the European Security Conference summit, Foreign Minister Chiao Kuan-hua's address to the U.N. General Assembly on 26 September 1975 emphasized the growing world danger of superpower-initiated war—especially from the Soviet Union. Chiao showed concern over possible gains for Soviet-sponsored détente following the Helsinki summit meeting, and amplified China's stand against the superpowers and in support of the developing third world countries on specific issues.

Sharply rebutting superpower claims of an "irreversible process of détente," Chiao stressed the enhanced danger of a "new world war" stemming from U.S.-Soviet world rivalry, voicing a formulation that "whether war gives rise to revolution or revolution prevents war," the future will be "bright." In 1974, by contrast, Chiao had stressed the then prevalent PRC view that revolution, not superpower war, was the "main" international trend, and he had been more sanguine that world popular opinion had successfully "seen through" the "smokescreen" of superpower détente. The foreign minister showed special concern over "deceptive" Soviet détente propaganda following the Helsinki summit, bluntly warning that "it would be dangerous indeed" to "be so naive as to believe in the Soviet propaganda." Chiao designated the Soviet Union as the major threat to peace, asserting that "the danger of war comes mainly from the wildly ambitious social imperialism"—the first time this charge had been made in authoritative Chinese media.

Though Chiao had ignored Moscow's Asian security plan in his 1974 speech, this time he accused Moscow of drumming up support for the plan so as to "fill the vacuum" left by the United States in Asia—a charge in line with other recent comments. Linking Soviet designs in Europe and Asia, Chiao added a unique charge that Moscow was also using propaganda on Asian security to conceal its prime objective of gaining control of Europe. Underlining this point, he reaffirmed the past Chinese judgment that Moscow was making a "feint to the east while attacking in the west."

Without mentioning Asian states by name, Chiao lauded Asian resistance to superpower "hegemony," hailing particularly the Southeast Asian states' efforts to create a regional zone of peace, "new progress" against hegemonism in South Asia (an apparent allusion to the rise of an anti-Soviet government in Bangladesh during August 1975), and the Iran-Iraq accord in early 1975 assisting the growth of the Persian Gulf states' unity against outside interference. Chiao claimed that the Soviet Asian security plan's alleged provision for recognition of existing frontiers was designed to legalize Soviet occupation of the territory of "some Asian countries" and to support "one Asian country"—meaning India—in violating its neighbors' boundaries.

Chiao's new charge that the Soviet Union was the most

dangerous source of war was underlined in a *Red Flag* article signed by Liang Hsiao and broadcast by Peking radio on 14 October 1975. The article detailed Soviet "hegemonism" in its relations with other countries and highlighted a new Chinese thesis that the Soviet Union's internal system makes it the more dangerous and aggressive of the two superpowers. The author asserted flatly that real change in its aggressive policies will require a fundamental change in the USSR's economic and political system, not merely changes in Soviet leadership or policy.

Liang described Moscow as a "latecomer" to the world imperialists' "feast" eager to make up for lost time and stated that the Soviet system of "state monopoly capitalism" made it the more formidable enemy. According the Liang, the Soviet system is "more monopolistic, more concentrated, and more tightly controlled" and therefore the Soviets are "more brutal in their aggression and expansion abroad." While acknowledging Soviet economic and technological inferiority to the United States, Liang stated that the USSR's ability to squeeze out surplus wealth to militarize the Soviet economy made it equally formidable militarily.

The article concluded with a discussion of internal forces and world forces opposed to Moscow's ambitions, noting especially that the third world—"the main force combatting imperialism"—had come to see more clearly the "true colors of the Soviet social imperialists" and was "increasingly directing its struggle against this deadly enemy." It also cited evidence of "new advances" by the developed second world countries against Moscow's policies, concluding that Soviet social imperialism, though outwardly fierce, is weak internally and a true "paper tiger."

Chinese criticism of Western "appeasement" of the "wildly expansionist" Soviet Union under the cover of détente received new impetus in response to the dismissal of U.S.

Defense Secretary Schlesinger. A 7 November 1975 NCNA dispatch reported critical U.S. and foreign comment on the firing. NCNA carefully refrained from comment in its own name, but the dispatch departed from Peking's past circumspect treatment of the U.S. administration by replaying comments which focused on the firing of Schlesinger as a clear sign of the Ford administration's determination to speed up détente with the Soviet Union and which criticized the decision as detrimental to U.S. national security.

The NCNA dispatch focused on the Schlesinger firing as an indication of the determination of the president and the secretary of state to "ease tensions" with Moscow; significantly, it did not follow the heretofore standard Chinese media practice of noting U.S. leaders' countervailing determination to resolutely maintain their country's security interests against alleged Soviet encroachment. NCNA replayed British press comment calling Kissinger the "arch-architect" of détente with Moscow. Again citing the British press, NCNA quoted the observation that President Ford's decision to release Schlesinger while retaining Kissinger "shows clearly which side he takes in the argument about détente."

NCNA reported comments by Senator Jackson and others praising Schlesinger and criticizing his dismissal as "a loss to the nation . . . in the pursuit of a prudent defense and foreign policy ." It cited statements that the firing had upset Western European leaders and could weaken NATO's strength against the Warsaw Pact. The dispatch replayed Soviet and U.S. comment highlighting Moscow's pleasure over Schlesinger's departure and speculating that "the shuffle in Washington will certainly be regarded by the Kremlin as a step in the right direction." It concluded by citing *Washington Post* reports that the Schlesinger dismissal would broaden the "already widening debate in the United

States over the pros and cons of détente with the Soviet Union."

The report was a clear departure from a then-standard practice of the Chinese media. Peking in recent years had rarely reported U.S. cabinet changes and it had invariably avoided replaying comments critical of such shifts. For instance, Peking was not known to have reported Schlesinger's 2 July 1973 appointment as defense secretary. The Chinese did note Secretary Kissinger's takeover in the State Department and William Rogers' departure in a terse, four-sentence September 1973 NCNA report. The resignation of former President Nixon and the inauguration of President Ford was also handled circumspectly with a brief 9 August 1974 NCNA dispatch.

On the same day that NCNA reported Schlesinger's dismissal, it carried two "international reference material" articles explaining respectively the significance of the 1938 Munich agreement and the 1940 Dunkirk evacuation to the Chinese domestic audience. The articles were also published in *People's Daily* and broadcast by Peking radio. The articles focused on the disastrous results of the Munich "policy of appeasement" followed by the British and French leaders in "conniving with the aggressive acts" of the fascists in order "to divert" the "spearhead of aggression toward the east." One report concluded by noting that "since then, people have often described similar schemes by several major powers in conniving at aggression and betraying other countries as a 'Munich' or a 'Munich Plot.' " Recent NCNA replays of foreign comment had highlighted those labeling the East-West agreement signed at the Helsinki European Security Conference in August 1975 as a new "Munich," as well as characterizations of Brezhnev playing the Hitler role at that conference. The implications of the Peking media's juxtaposition of reports on Schlesinger's dismissal with those on the

1938 Munich agreement centered on the fact that Peking viewed the Ford administration's dismissal of Schlesinger in an attempt to ease U.S.-Soviet tensions as similar to Chamberlain's efforts to appease Hitler at the Munich Conference in 1938.

Stepping up its antidétente propaganda efforts, Peking's year-end comment on foreign affairs dwelt on Soviet "expansion" against the West. It was highlighted by a comprehensive 25 December 1975 *People's Daily* article attributed to Jen Ku-ping, a signature that had appeared frequently over authoritative Chinese comment during 1975. The assessment of world developments was most notable for sharpened criticism of the policies of the Soviet Union, depicted as the "main" danger to international peace. The United States was still seen by Peking as strategically equal to the USSR, but as on the defensive in the face of a surging "offensive strategy" of the USSR. As in comment at the end of 1974, which had also been capped by a Jen Ku-ping *People's Daily* article, a Soviet threat to China was not stressed while Europe was portrayed as the target of Soviet ambitions.

The current Jen Ku-ping commentary flatly called the USSR "the most dangerous source of war," in contrast to his review of 1974 which labeled both superpowers as a potential source of world war. The commentary this time also departed from the previous year's more evenhanded critique of the policies of both the USSR and the United States by containing a scathing denouncement of Moscow's strategy and a softpedaling of past charges against Washington. This pattern was also followed in several late December NCNA reviews of 1975 developments which muffled past years' criticism of U.S. actions in East Asia, Africa, Cyprus, and other areas and vividly portrayed the USSR as the primary danger to peace in all regions, even in such unlikely places as the Caribbean and South America.

The bulk of one article focused on the "intensified" superpower arms race and rivalry in Europe, stressing China's arguments against Soviet détente policies. Specifically ridiculing the Helsinki summit accord on European security signed in August 1975 and the November 1974 U.S.-Soviet Vladivostok accord on strategic arms, the article highlighted the alleged futility of attempting to limit Soviet ambitions with such "scrap paper." It observed that despite past disarmament agreements, the USSR had virtually closed the "gap" in the nuclear arms race with the United States and was in the "superior position" in the field of conventional arms. It took unusual pains to detail Soviet designs on Europe, noting that three quarters of Soviet forces are deployed there and that the Soviets are presently "baring their fangs and showing their claws," bringing about a "sabre-rattling and tense situation" along the western front.

Peking's anti-Soviet comment at the start of the new year echoed these themes. Peking's attacks on the Soviet Union were highlighted by the republication in the 1 January 1976 *People's Daily* of the two poems attacking Soviet revisionism written by Mao in 1965. A 2 January 1976 *People's Daily* article, signed by the prominent anti-Soviet commentator Fan Hsiu-chu, explained one of the poems—entitled "Two Birds"—as a blunt rebuke to the Khrushchev-Brezhnev policies of betraying national liberation struggles, negotiating strategic arms agreements with Washington, and restoring capitalism in the Soviet Union. Stressing the continued relevance of the poem, the article charged that the Brezhnev leadership had become even more menacing and aggressive than Khrushchev's. It reiterated the Chinese thesis that the Soviet Union is not only the chief source of war in the present world, but also "the most ferocious enemy of the people of the world" and "the biggest international exploiter and oppressor."

A lengthy 3 January year-end commentary from NCNA reiterated the Chinese contention that the USSR is more aggressive and oppressive than the traditional imperialist states because of the more centralized and controlled structure of Soviet "state monopoly capitalism." The commentary used unusually strong language in attacking the Soviet leaders, charging that Khrushchev and Brezhnev were like Hitler, and characterizing them in extreme terms as having their hands "dripping with the blood of the people" of the USSR. NCNA devoted great attention to describing the massive Soviet war machine that had been built under Brezhnev's leadership, depicting Soviet "expansionism" as directed against U.S. interests, especially in Europe.

Peking pressed forward with its polemical campaign against the Soviets in a 27 January *People's Daily* article by Jen Ku-ping which warned that the Soviet Union is building up its military forces more rapidly than the United States. Jen Ku-ping restated the analysis of the Soviet system of "state monopoly capitalism" first set forth in the lengthy *Red Flag* article by Liang Hsiao in October 1975. Both articles held that the "capitalism" of the Soviet Union was more monopolistic and concentrated than that of a conventional imperialist state, and that it was the main factor motivating Soviet expansionism. Both articles portrayed the Soviet Union as taking the offensive against the United States, but Jen Ku-ping went on to charge that the Soviets are clamoring for "gaining mastery by striking first" and are prepared to "risk the beginning of a new world war."

In his October 1975 article, Liang Hsiao had stated that military expenditures by Moscow and Washington were nearly equal although the Soviet gross national product was only about half that of the United States. However, Jen Ku-ping painted a more dire picture charging that Soviet arms expansion and war preparations had "greatly surpassed the

United States" and that the Soviet military budget was "the biggest in the world." Jen echoed other authoritative Peking comment by claiming that the USSR had already gained the advantage over the United States in conventional weaponry. Elsewhere, he maintained that "due to a change in the balance of power between Soviet revisionism and the other superpower, social imperialism now has the wild ambition to contend for world hegemony by armed force."

Impact of PRC Leadership Changes, 1976

During the remainder of 1976, Chinese policies were dominated by the impact of major internal leadership changes. Premier Chou En-lai, NPC Chairman Chu Te, and CCP Chairman Mao Tse-tung died in January, June, and September, respectively; Teng Hsiao-ping was removed from his posts in April; and the four leftist Politburo members were arrested in October. Hua Kuo-feng was named to the posts of acting premier in February, premier in April, and CCP chairman in October. Yeh Chien-ying and Li Hsien-nien—Chinese Politburo members who had dropped from public view along with Teng Hsiao-peng following Chou's death in January—received unusual prominence in Chinese media following the purge of the four leftists in October.

Apparently in reaction to these major leadership shifts, Chinese spokesmen throughout the year repeatedly cautioned that the basic orientation of Chinese foreign policy would not change. However, there were signs that leaders in Peking were not in agreement on how PRC foreign policy should be carried out. Internal leadership politics in the fluid situation in Peking apparently spilled over into Chinese foreign policy, complicating the continuation of Peking's past pragmatic foreign approach.

The key tenets of Peking's foreign policy were reaffirmed

by China's new acting premier, Hua Kuo-feng, during his major diplomatic debut as host for former president Nixon in February 1976. The Chinese leadership's commitment to improve Sino-U.S. relations was underlined both by the cordial reception given the former president and Hua's remarks at a welcoming banquet on the 22nd. Hua's banquet statements included a call for greater vigilance against Soviet "expansionism," a theme which had likewise been pressed by Chinese spokesmen during President Ford's visit to China in December 1975.

Hua Kuo-feng's strong affirmation at the 22 February banquet of the importance of the Sino-U.S. rapprochement seemed to be calculated to allay concern that changes in the Chinese leadership during the then ongoing campaign against Teng Hsiao-ping might jeopardize the Sino-U.S. relationship. Hua echoed remarks by Teng Hsiao-ping at Teng's banquet for Ford in December 1975 when he restated Chinese support for the Shanghai communiqué, maintained there was common ground between the two countries, and recalled Nixon's role in opening relations with China. As Teng had done during Ford's visit in December, Hua warned his audience that the Soviet Union was "the main source of war," stressing that strengthened world unity and resolve were "the only realistic and effective way to cope" with Soviet expansionism. Hua did not repeat Teng's explicit December attack on "détente," but cited a June 1972 Nixon warning that "idealism" was no way to stem international aggression.

Peking's continuing anti-Soviet bias was evident as the *People's Daily* repeatedly denounced Brezhnev during the Twenty-Fifth Communist Party of the Soviet Union (CPSU) Congress in February 1976. Peking's first comment, explicitly timed with the 24 February opening of the Soviet congress, came in a lengthy 23 February *People's Daily* article signed by Hsaio Lou lambasting the Brezhnev regime's foreign and domestic policies in strong and personal terms. The article was widely broadcast to domestic and foreign audiences, including Russian listeners on the 24th. (Peking media had not taken the trouble in 1971 to offer such criticism of the Soviet leadership during the Twenty-Fourth CPSU Congress.)

The *People's Daily* article condemned in strong terms the policies followed by the Brezhnev regime in the five years between the twenty-fourth and twenty-fifth Soviet congresses, claiming that Brezhnev engaged in "bankrupt" economic measures, intensified social oppression within the USSR, and expanded Soviet aggression abroad. Hsiao Lou was unusually personal in ridiculing Brezhnev, claiming for example that Brezhnev's receiving the military rank of army general the previous year had made him a "laughing stock" before the world.

People's Daily also gave notable stress to the "isolated," "weakened," and "tottering" position of the Brezhnev regime, asserting that it had reinforced "social-fascist dictatorship" within the USSR in order to deal with the "unremitting" and "constantly increased" resistance of the Soviet people. The article emphasized failures in Soviet "expansionism" abroad, noting that while Moscow's "malignant" arms development had made the USSR the world's most dangerous source of war, Soviet foreign policy had been stymied over such critical issues as the SALT arms talks, the U.S.-Soviet trade deal, and the conference of European communist parties.

Peking media had led up to the congress with an increase in Chinese criticism over the previous two weeks which focused on alleged failures in Brezhnev's agricultural and economic policies and denounced his leadership's alleged suppression of national minorities and dissidents within the

USSR. For instance, a 21 February Peking radio signed article beamed to Chinese domestic listeners claimed that the "perverted actions" of the "Brezhnev clique" in Soviet agriculture reflected their efforts to "rapaciously suck the blood" of Soviet peasants; a 14 February NCNA commentary equated Moscow's alleged support of "great Russian chauvinism" and "pan-Slavism" with Hitler's "great Germanism"; and a 21 February NCNA article portrayed the pre-congress leadership shakeup in the Ukraine as the latest expression of the Brezhnev regime's oppression of national minorities in the USSR.

Peking was also more strident than in the past in encouraging Soviet workers and dissidents to rise up against Brezhnev's rule, and it sharply condemned Moscow's use of internal security organs to control antiregime figures. A 23 February NCNA correspondent's commentary described in unusually lurid terms alleged atrocities committed in Soviet concentration camps, claiming that the Soviet regime engaged in widespread torture and brutality in imitation of the practices of Hitler's "Nazi death camps."

A 10 March *People's Daily* article by Jen Ku-ping capped the heavy outpouring of Chinese invective against Brezhnev's 24 February report at the CPSU Congress. The article focused criticism on Brezhnev's claim to be continuing the "peace program" begun at the Twenty-Fourth CPSU Congress in 1971, charging that Soviet "aggression and expansion" over the past five years clearly belied Brezhnev's repeated, "hackneyed tunes of détente." Other Chinese media commentaries continued to criticize Brezhnev on specific domestic and foreign issues, with the result that the volume of anti-Soviet comment maintained an unusually high level for four weeks following the congress.

Jen Ku-ping caustically ridiculed Brezhnev's détente proposals as "filled with fine words and claptrap aimed at impressing people," and claimed that Soviet peace plans were simply efforts "to sell dog meat as mutton" which "can only make people sick." He asserted that during the five years since the Soviet "peace program," Moscow had rapidly expanded its armaments, had "caught up with and even surpassed the United States in some respects in both conventional and nuclear weapons," and had become "the most dangerous source of war today." The article compared Brezhnev's détente proposals with Hitler's disarmament plans prior to World War II, warning that the "historical lesson of the 1930s is of immediate significance."

On specific issues mentioned in Brezhnev's report, the article claimed that "it is indeed ridiculous" for Brezhnev to brag about the Helsinki Conference on Security and Cooperation in Europe (CSCE) summit last summer since "this short-lived fraud" had been fully "exposed" over the past six months. The article asserted that Brezhnev's call for safeguarding security in Asia demonstrated that Moscow remained determined to overcome the resistance of Asian countries and to "impose" its "Asian security system." It went on to claim that Brezhnev's call for an international treaty on the nonuse of force was merely designed "to add new smell" to the Soviet peace program.

China's continued strong interest in developing anti-Soviet trends in other key areas of the world was seen during a 3-9 May 1976 visit to China by British Foreign Secretary Anthony Crosland and a 28 April-5 May 1976 visit to China by Prime Minister Robert Muldoon of New Zealand. During the British visit, Peking comment underscored China's strong interest in promoting closer relations with the major Western European powers and greater Western European unity against Soviet "hegemonism." Chinese statements during Muldoon's visit stressed Sino–New Zealander agreement to oppose Soviet "expansionism" in Asia and Oceania.

The activities of the British delegation generally followed the pattern of the visit in November 1975 by French Foreign Minister Sauvagnargues—the previously most recent visit of a high-level delegation from a major Western European state. The British group held talks with high-level Chinese officials, including Premier Hua Kuo-feng on 6 May and Foreign Trade Minister Li Chiang on the previous day, was feted at a welcoming banquet hosted by Foreign Minister Chiao Kuan-hua on 4 May, hosted a reciprocal banquet attended by Chiao on the 6th, and toured Chinese provincial cities after leaving Peking on 7 May.

Chiao Kuan-hua's assessment of the European situation in his remarks at the welcoming banquet followed the anti-Soviet line he had used during a welcoming banquet for Sauvagnargues the previous November. He routinely emphasized that Europe remained the "focus" of U.S.-Soviet international rivalry, stressed that the main threat to Europe came from Soviet expansion, and lauded what he saw as a growing tendency among Western Europeans to see through Soviet peace blandishments and to heighten preparations to defend their national security. Chiao underlined Peking's avowed support for closer Western European unity by declaring that such solidarity "in the face of hegemonism" represented "the dictate of history," and he asserted that China was ready to "cooperate" with the Western Europeans "in a common effort against hegemonism."

Chiao's remarks at the reciprocal banquet on the 6th duly noted continued Chinese differences with Britain but stressed that improved bilateral understanding had been achieved as a result of Crosland's stay. He was optimistic regarding prospects for Sino-British relations, emphasizing that Crosland's visit had made a "new contribution" to improving bilateral ties and that there were "good prospects" for further growth.

New Zealand's Muldoon was greeted on his arrival on 28
April by Premier Hua Kuo-feng and Foreign Minister Chiao
Kuan-hua and welcomed by a *People's Daily* editorial that
day. Hua hosted a banquet for Muldoon on the 29th and held
talks with him on the 29th and 30th. The prime minister had
a "friendly" talk with Mao Tse-tung on the 30th and
participated in Peking's May Day festivities. After observing
the formal exchange of letters on shipping trade and hosting
a reciprocal banquet on the 1st, Muldoon departed Peking
on the 2nd for Shanghai, Soochow, and Canton before
leaving China on 5 May. While no joint communiqué was
released after the visit (there had been one following the
November 1973 Peking visit Prime Minister Whitlam of
Australia), the atmospherics throughout Muldoon's visit
were correct and closely paralleled those of the Whitlam
visit.

Speeches by Hua Kuo-feng at the banquets on 29 April and
1 May dwelt on the issue of the alleged threat from the Soviet
Union. On the 29th Hua asserted that it was a matter of
"natural concern" to both China and New Zealand that as
"one superpower has been forced to contract, the other
superpower has grabbed the chance to step up its infiltration
and expansion in the Asia-Pacific region." He expressed
gratification that the countries of Southeast Asia and Oceania have become aware of the "danger" and were "strengthening their cooperation in a united struggle" to meet it. In
his 1 May reciprocal banquet, Hua observed that while the
two countries held different views on "certain issues," they
shared "much common ground on major issues of the world
today," particularly on the necessity of vigilance against
"the superpower that goes in for sham détente and real
expansionism."

While Hua did not attack the USSR by name, the 28 April
People's Daily editorial explicitly portrayed the present New

Zealand government as one that stressed "vigilance against the expansion of Soviet social imperialism in Asia and the Pacific and Indian oceans." Efforts by the New Zealand government to strengthen joint defense with Australia and enhance cooperation with other Southeast Asian countries were evaluated by the editorial as "favorable to the struggle against hegemonism" in the area.

Following Mao's death and the arrest of the four leftist Politburo members, the *People's Daily* on 10 October 1976 strongly reaffirmed China's anti-Soviet credentials by calling on the Chinese people to join the masses in the world to wage "protracted struggle" against the USSR. Authored by Jen Ku-ping and entitled "Resolutely Combat Soviet Modern Revisionism," the article was especially emphatic in stating that China had an inescapable, enduring obligation to oppose the massive "crimes" of the Brezhnev leadership, and that the future course of world history depended on this effort. Chinese opposition to Soviet revisionism, according to Jen Ku-ping, had a "direct bearing" on the "success or defeat" of international revolution and the "liberation of oppressed nations and people the world over." He made it clear that Peking's "protracted struggle" to wipe Soviet revisionism "from the face of the earth" was not merely an ideological conflict but would involve strong Chinese opposition to Soviet foreign policy. "It is necessary to oppose the acts of aggression and expansion of Soviet social imperialism," he declared, adding that "today the struggle against modern revisionism is closely connected with the struggle of the world's people against imperialism and social imperialism."

In building his case against the Soviet leadership, Jen claimed that the "crimes" committed by the "Khrushchev-Brezhnev clique" in betraying Marxism-Leninism and world revolution were "a thousand times more serious" than those committed by "all revisionists in the past." Jen charged that Brezhnev had repeatedly outdone Khrushchev as a revisionist and imperialist, noting that Brezhnev "completed the evolution from capitalist restoration to social imperialism in the USSR, strengthened the Soviets' fascist dictatorship at home and intensified aggression and expansion on a worldwide scale."

Under Brezhnev, Jen went on, the Soviet Union had become one of the world's "biggest exploiters and oppressors" and "the most ferocious enemy of the people the world over and the most dangerous source of war." He cited as evidence a long list of Soviet "crimes of aggression" abroad, including a rare Chinese reference to Brezhnev's alleged use of "armed provocations against China." Since Brezhnev consistently hides Soviet "expansion" under cloaks of "socialism" and "détente," Jen argued, the Soviets are as "deceitful" as they are "dangerous." He concluded that it is therefore the "inescapable obligation" of all genuine Marxist-Leninists to relentlessly "strip them of their disguise" and "expose their real features."

Despite the general impression of agreement among the Chinese leadership over Chinese foreign policy during 1976, there were occasional signs in the Chinese media that the leftist leaders disagreed with certain aspects of the foreign policy carried out by moderate leaders like Chou En-lai and Teng Hsiao-ping. Thus, for example, leftist leaders who were particularly prominent during the campaign against Teng Hsiao-ping in mid-1976 used their influence in propaganda circles to push lines different from those advocated by the moderates. In particular they criticized Teng's advocacy of increased foreign trade, especially with the West; they adopted a harder line than the moderates on the Taiwan issue; and they were more critical of the United States.

Evidence of leftist disagreement with Teng's moderate

foreign trade policy was seen in NCNA comment marking the 15 May 1976 closing of China's semiannual Canton trade fair which criticized Teng Hsiao-ping's "slavish comprador" foreign trade policy and gave unusual stress to the primary importance of the principles of independence and self-reliance in China's national economic development. NCNA reaffirmed China's continued interest in importing foreign goods "in a planned way" but, unlike comment on fair closings in May and November 1975 (when Teng was in power), the current propaganda did not advocate that China learn from foreigners, cater to foreign tastes in the manufacture and shipping of Chinese exports, or increase its foreign trade.

A 16 May NCNA commentary on the Canton fair stressed the primacy of Mao's line on "keeping to the principles of independence and self-reliance" while trading with foreign nations on the basis of principles of "equality and mutual benefit." Another NCNA report on the 15th emphasized that the number and quality of Chinese goods on display at the fair vividly demonstrated the rewards of China's adhering to self-reliance. By contrast, NCNA commentaries on the fair the previous November and May had given only passing attention to the need for independence and self-reliance. The 1975 comment had called on Chinese workers to seek the guidance of foreigners in order to improve the quality and value of China's exports, hailed the "remarkable changes" made in China's export trade, and flatly asserted that "China's foreign trade will continue to increase"—themes absent in current comment.

The recent comment did caution that China's stress on self-reliance did not mean that "we lock our door against the world and refuse to develop foreign trade or to introduce from abroad certain techniques and equipment really useful to China." NCNA claimed defensively that the present policy was "entirely different" from that advocated by Teng Hsiao-ping, which it said "depended on foreign techniques and equipment for developing China's economy so as to make imperialism and social imperialism gain control of the development of China's economy and reduce China to their economic appendage." It added that Teng had opposed the principles of independence and self-reliance, and had pushed a philosophy of "servility to things foreign" and the doctrine of "trailing behind at a snail's pace."

Teng Hsiao-ping's alleged errors in foreign trade policy had been cited in earlier Peking propaganda. Thus, for example, a 28 March 1976 *People's Daily* editorial attacking "the capitalist roader in the party" had accused him of attempting to oppose independence and self-reliance and advocating a "slavish comprador philosophy" and the doctrine of "trailing behind at a snail's pace." Similar charges were reviewed at length in an article by Fang Hai in the April 1976 *Red Flag* entitled "Criticize the Slavish Comprador Philosophy." The article charged that the "unrepentant capitalist roader" had "openly advocated entrusting the desire to develop production and technology to foreign countries," shouting that "we must exchange many things for the newest and best foreign equipment."

On the Taiwan issue there was no notable change in Peking's moderate media line, but newly prominent leftist leaders—especially Vice Premier Chang Chun-chiao—used the opportunities of meetings with U.S. visitors to voice a strident line on Taiwan. For example, it was Chang Chun-chiao who particularly impressed Senator Hugh Scott on 13 July 1976 with the firmness of Peking's intention to use military force to liberate Taiwan if necessary. Chang's approach recalled the harsh Chinese propaganda line on Taiwan in early 1974, when leftist leaders' views had been prominent during the massive ideological campaign against

Confucius and Lin Piao.

Leftist-inspired criticism of the United States appeared at the time of Mao's death when the Chinese media, for the first time in four years, began citing numerous statements Mao had made critical of the United States. References to Mao's statements attacking U.S. policies during the 1946-1949 Chinese civil war and criticizing the alleged oppression of communists and blacks in the United States during the 1950s and 1960s were featured in a 23 September NCNA report on popular mourning of Mao's death in the United States. And similar criticism Mao had made had been recalled in NCNA commentaries on 13 August and on 12 September. References to such statements of Mao were common in Peking propaganda prior to the Sino-U.S. rapprochement in 1972, but were not known to have appeared in national Chinese media since then.

The lengthy 23 September NCNA report on the American "people's" mourning for Mao stressed Mao's role as a consistent supporter of the "struggle" and "revolutionary cause" of the "oppressed" American people, and gave only passing attention to Mao's contribution to building Sino-American "friendship." The report—carried by NCNA's Chinese and English services and broadcast by Peking radio's domestic and international services—highlighted remarks made by an unnamed spokesman for a U.S. leftist group who recalled Mao's attack on U.S. government policies in an August 1946 interview with U.S. journalist Anna Louise Strong. NCNA noted the spokesman's comment that Mao had "laid stress on differentiating between the American people and the handful of U.S. rulers," and it cited the spokesman's reference to Mao's 17 January 1959 message to William Z. Foster of the U.S. Communist Party as proof of Mao's backing for "the communist movement in the United States." NCNA also claimed that "many Afro-Americans" viewed Mao's 1963 and 1968 statements on the civil rights movement in the United States as vivid reminders of Mao's "solidarity with the Afro-American struggle."

A 12 September NCNA commentary, calling on third world countries to refuse Soviet foreign aid, compared Soviet foreign aid to the allegedly self-serving U.S. aid efforts in China during the Chinese civil war. It charged that the 1949 U.S. State Department white paper on China had shown that the United States had used food aid as a means to put China "under U.S. control as a colony," and it recalled that Mao had led the Chinese in condemning U.S. aid while stressing Chinese "self-reliance."

A 13 August NCNA commentary similarly likened current Soviet foreign aid policies to U.S. aid efforts in China during the late 1940s. It recalled Mao's harsh attack against U.S. aid in his famous 1949 article marking the departure of Leighton Stuart, the last U.S. ambassador to China, and it noted Mao's warning in that article that money and aid are given by imperialists only on the condition that the recipient country follows their directions.

In late 1975, immediately prior to Chou En-lai's death, there appeared indirect evidence of Chinese leadership disagreement over policy toward the Soviet Union. The evidence centered around the December 1975 release by the PRC government of a Soviet helicopter and crew that had been captured inside the Chinese border in March 1974. The capture had coincided with an upsurge of harsh Chinese attacks against the Soviet Union which were associated with the massive anti-Confucius campaign fostered by the four leftist Politburo members. At that time, Chinese propaganda organs—presumably under leftist influence—had stated flatly that the captured Soviets were guilty of spying. However, the December 1975 Chinese announcement of the Soviets' release—made at a time when moderates led by Teng

Hsiao-ping maintained predominant power—took the unprecedented step of contradicting the 1974 Chinese judgment, asserting that the Soviets were not spying. Although the precise motivation for taking this unusual step remains unclear, the implications are that Teng and his supporters strongly disagreed with the arrest of the helicopter crew—an action which had needlessly exacerbated Sino-Soviet tension over the sensitive border issue.

The announcement was a remarkable reversal of Peking's consistent contention, proclaimed officially in a 23 March 1974 PRC Foreign Ministry statement, that a "thorough investigation" had established a "conclusive" case that the flight was part of the longstanding Soviet policy of spying against China. The 1974 statement had rebuked Soviet authorities for trying to cover up the crime by claiming that the intrusion into China was unintentional. Since 1974 Chinese media had continued to refer to the "spy mission" from time to time. The last known reference was on 1 October 1975 when comment marking the twentieth anniversary of the founding of Sinkiang Province praised the provincial border defense units there for capturing the Soviet helicopter and its crew.

The 27 December 1975 NCNA report of the release was carried textually in the agency's Chinese and English transmissions and broadcast widely by Peking radio to foreign as well as domestic audiences. The announcement said cryptically that Vice Foreign Minister Yu Chan had informed Soviet Ambassador Tolstikov that the helicopter and its crew were being returned since "after investigation" the Chinese public security organs "consider credible the Soviet crew members' statement about the unintentional flight into China."

Part Two
Recent PRC Policy on Specific Foreign Issues

Introduction

As the new Chinese leadership headed by CCP Chairman Hua Kuo-feng and prominent protégés of Chou En-lai like CCP Vice Chairman Yeh Chien-ying and Vice Premier Li Hsien-nien entered 1977, there appeared to be little likelihood that Peking would depart significantly from the pragmatic, geopolitical foreign policy laid out by Chou En-lai earlier in the decade. Most importantly, the Chinese leaders remained preoccupied with such fundamental domestic problems as the completion of the purge of party members associated with the four arrested leftist Politburo members and the reestablishment of a unified Chinese party leadership. In this context, major initiatives in foreign affairs appeared unlikely. As a result, one can gain a solid perspective on China's current approach to important foreign policy questions by examining in detail the development of China's policy toward these issues in recent years.

Sino-Soviet Relations

Chinese and Soviet public statements since the start of the Sino-Soviet border talks in Peking in October 1969 have demonstrated a deep mutual hostility which has blocked significant improvement in Sino-Soviet relations. The accomplishments of the Peking negotiations and other Sino-Soviet efforts to improve relations have been limited. Both sides have generally refrained from aggravating the military confrontation along the Sino-Soviet border, which had been the scene of serious armed clashes earlier in 1969. In addition, the two sides have managed to reestablish and maintain a modicum of decorum in the conduct of routine diplomatic and trade relations.

Over the past eight years, both countries have taken initiatives which have temporarily improved the atmosphere—if not the substance—of Sino-Soviet relations. The initiatives have been designed primarily for self-serving purposes. Both Moscow and Peking have used them to portray an image of reasonableness and to avoid the appearance of being the intransigent party in the dispute.

1. During the first weeks of the Peking negotiations, both sides muted polemics and Soviet spokesmen were unusually conciliatory in talking about China. On 27 October 1969, Brezhnev optimistically predicted that Sino-Soviet relations would improve and made an unusual reference to Chou En-lai as a "comrade"—a term implicitly denoting Soviet interest in party relations with China.

2. In late 1970, both sides moderated polemics and agreed to resume ambassadorial-level diplomatic relations and formal trade ties. Moscow followed in January 1971 with its first major initiative in the Peking talks, a proposal concern-

ing a mutual agreement to renounce the use of force. In March, Chou En-lai took the highly unusual step of granting a four-hour private interview with the chief Soviet negotiator and the Soviet ambassador.

3. The Soviet Union made a series of gestures toward China following the death of Mao Tse-tung in September 1976. Soviet polemics against China were halted, Brezhnev sent two messages to Chinese leaders, and the chief Soviet negotiator returned to the Peking talks after an absence of eighteen months. Peking also reduced anti-Soviet polemics, but Chinese spokesmen soon made it clear that the Soviet gestures had not been accompanied by serious efforts to accommodate China's demands over basic questions in the Sino-Soviet dispute.

During the first year of the Peking talks, both sides used the negotiations, as well as normal diplomatic and propaganda channels, to initiate proposals which led to a resumption of ambassadorial-level relations and formal trade ties by late 1970. Over the next three years, Moscow tabled proposals at the talks regarding agreements on mutual nonuse of force and nonaggression, which were ostensibly designed to ease Sino-Soviet disagreement over the border. Peking rejected the Soviet initiatives and maintained consistently that Soviet troops had to be withdrawn from disputed border regions before serious negotiations on the border question could take place. The talks wore on without result and Sino-Soviet polemics gradually increased. By late 1973, the Peking negotiations and Sino-Soviet relations were at an impasse.

Moscow and Peking marked the start of the Peking talks with a halt in direct propaganda attacks against each other—a hiatus which lasted several weeks in China's case and several months in the case of the USSR. While Chinese leaders withheld comment on the border talks, high-level

Soviet spokesmen were optimistic about prospects for improved relations as a result of the negotiations. Moscow's first comment on the talks came in a 27 October 1969 speech by Brezhnev in which he voiced conciliatory hopes for a reduction in Sino-Soviet tensions. Brezhnev also suggested possible Soviet interest in party relations with China. He referred to Chou En-lai as "comrade"—a fraternal gesture not seen in Soviet comment on China since the Cultural Revolution.

Peking was dissatisfied with the Soviet position in the talks, however. Articles appearing in a Chinese-communist-controlled newspaper in Hong Kong in November 1969 and January 1970 complained that Moscow had refused to meet Peking's primary condition for the start of serious negotiations—the withdrawal of Soviet forces from disputed regions along the border. Peking media also began to occasionally attack the Soviet Union by name. The 1 January 1970 Chinese joint editorial contained the first authoritative Chinese criticism of Brezhnev since the Sino-Soviet talks began.

Soviet commentators gradually escalated complaints against China, reaching a high point in speeches by the three top Soviet leaders in June 1970. A 19 March *Pravda* article appearing under the authoritative byline "I. Aleksandrov" sharply criticized the Chinese for allegedly attempting to use the Chinese war preparations campaign to put pressure on the Soviet Union in the Peking talks. Brezhnev, Podgorny, and Kosygin, in speeches during the election campaign of the supreme Soviet in mid-June, charged that Chinese intransigence was blocking progress in Sino-Soviet relations. Typically, Kosygin on 10 June alleged that the Chinese were following a line which was not conducive to "any appreciable progress" in bilateral relations and noted that the Peking talks were "hampered through the fault of the

Chinese side." On 30 June, Moscow withdrew its chief negotiator at the Peking talks, ostensibly because of illness.

Chou En-lai made China appear less intransigent by taking the highly unusual step of sending an official message to Kosygin on 13 June 1970 expressing sorrow over recent floods and earthquakes in the USSR. Two months later, Peking agreed to resume ambassadorial relations with Moscow—an accord first disclosed by Kosygin during an interview with an Indian newspaper on 10 August. On 15 August, the newly appointed chief Soviet negotiator to the Peking talks, Deputy Foreign Minister Ilichev, arrived in China to resume formal negotiations.

Brezhnev followed with the most conciliatory Soviet assessment of China since the early period of the Peking talks. Speaking in Alma Alta on 28 August 1971, Brezhnev did not blame China for the fact that the Peking talks were "going slowly" and he stressed instead that Moscow was "not losing hope" and would "continue to display a constructive and patient approach" in the hope that the Chinese "will respond in the same way." Brezhnev called for a broader accommodation than simply the restoration of correct bilateral state relations and he hinted—as he had done the previous October—that Moscow was interested in party relations with China. In particular, he asserted that the Soviet party and government were ready to contribute "not only" to the normalization of state relations "but also the restoration of good neighborliness and friendship between the Soviet and Chinese peoples and the unity of their efforts in the struggle against imperialism and reaction."

Sino-Soviet state relations received a boost forward in late 1970 following the arrival of Soviet Ambassador Tolstikov in Peking during October and Chinese Ambassador Liu Hsin-chuan in Moscow during November. On 22 November, a new trade agreement, the first since 1967, was signed.

Moscow used this favorable backdrop to offer its first major initiative in the Peking talks—a proposal for mutual nonuse of force—which was tabled on 15 January 1971. The proposal was not referred to publicly until Brezhev talked about it during a March 1972 speech. Peking reportedly showed little interest in the Soviet offer, but Chou En-lai maintained an image of Chinese reasonableness when he received Ilichev and Tolstikov for a private meeting on 21 March. Soviet media reported the session two days later, but Peking remained silent on it. Moscow's report said that "questions of interest to both sides" were discussed. Western press reports from Peking said that the meeting lasted four hours.

In July 1971 the Chinese invited the American president to visit China, marking the formal start of the Chinese international strategy designed to unite with the United States and other capitalist and third world countries against what Peking saw as its main enemy—the USSR. Significantly, the Nixon visit in February 1972 was capped by the Shanghai communiqué which noted both sides' pledge to oppose international "hegemony"—a codeword used by the Chinese to denote the Soviet Union.

Recognizing that it could do little to impede the Sino-U.S. rapprochement, the Soviet Union adopted a wait-and-see attitude regarding the implications for Moscow as a result of the Nixon visit to China. Typically, Brezhnev reserved judgment in a speech on 22 March 1972 as to whether Nixon's visit would affect Sino-Soviet relations, and he declared that Moscow would continue to await Peking's reply to "specific and constructive" Soviet proposals in the Peking negotiations.

Over the next year, Moscow showed increasing dissatisfaction with Peking's unmoving stand in the negotiations and its developing international strategy against the USSR. Brezhnev harshly criticized the Chinese on 21 December

1972, accusing Peking of laying claim to Soviet territory, sabotaging efforts on East-West détente, and attempting to "split" the communist camp. He claimed that Peking's sole criterion on any major issue was to inflict the greatest possible damage on the interests of the USSR.

On 19 July 1973 Moscow took the unusual action of announcing the departure of Ilichev from Peking that day, ostensibly for "official duties." (The negotiator was not to return to China for almost a year.) Soviet comment later revealed that in early July 1973 Ilichev had offered a new Soviet proposal over the border problem which had been rebuffed by the Chinese. The proposal involved an agreement on mutual nonaggression. Subsequently, a 7 August authoritative commentary in *Pravda* and a speech by Brezhnev on 15 August placed full blame on the Chinese for the stalemate in relations. Chou En-Lai responded during his 24 August speech to the Tenth CCP Congress. Castigating "the Brezhnev renegade clique" for "talking a lot of nonsense" about Sino-Soviet relations, Chou asked sarcastically "must China give away all territory north of the Great Wall to the Soviet revisionists" in order to demonstrate willingness to improve Sino-Soviet relations?

Peking held the initiative in Sino-Soviet relations over the next three years. For reasons unrelated to problems in Sino-Soviet relations, the Chinese took actions which seriously exacerbated Sino-Soviet tensions. Thus, for example, the anti-Confucius campaign fostered by leftist leaders in China during early 1974 prompted the Chinese to sharply increase polemics against the Soviet Union. At this time the Chinese also took the highly unusual step of arresting as "spies" a number of Soviet diplomats and three Soviet border guards. The arrest of the latter resulted in an exchange of strong protests which led to the first major crisis along the Sino-Soviet border since the armed clashes of 1969.

A year later the Chinese launched a major propaganda campaign designed to warn against Moscow's alleged desire to start a "new world war" in order to gain control of all world regions. Peking's propaganda campaign was accelerated during 1975 and 1976 in order to encourage an anti-Soviet international balance in the wake of the U.S. defeats in Indochina and acceleration of Soviet-fostered détente in Europe. Soviet spokesmen repeatedly complained at this time that they had little choice but to wait for a basic change in the makeup of the Chinese leadership. Moscow predicted that "healthy forces" would emerge in Peking following Mao's demise. In the interim, Soviet comment offered voluminous self-serving accounts of Moscow's past gestures and proposals allegedly designed to improve Sino-Soviet relations.

Mao's death on 9 September 1976 presented the Soviets with a new opportunity. Having consistently viewed Mao as the main instigator of Peking's anti-Soviet line, Moscow responded to his death with a series of public gestures ostensibly designed to show the post-Mao leaders in China that the Soviet Union was prepared to seek an accommodation of Sino-Soviet differences.

1. Moscow media stopped past criticism of China. The closest Moscow came to criticizing China in the next four months was to note in an disapproving way that Peking's propaganda continued to criticize Soviet policies.

2. Brezhnev sent a CPSU message of condolences on Mao's death—the first Soviet party message to be sent to China in a decade. Brezhnev followed with a CPSU message congratulating Hua Kuo-feng on his appointment as the new Chinese party chairman in October.

3. Soviet media gave unusual attention to China's 1 October 1976 National Day. Although *Pravda* articles on the anniversary had previously been authored by ordinary com-

mentators, the article this time appeared under the authoritative byline I. Aleksandrov. The article echoed prevailing Soviet comment in recalling Soviet aid to China during the 1950s and Soviet efforts to normalize relations and ease Sino-Soviet border tensions since the start of the Peking talks in 1969.

4. In late November, the Soviets sent Ilichev back to China after an absence of 18 months.

Peking formally disavowed any interest in the Soviet gestures, but also demonstrated that China's approach toward the Soviet Union would not be as strident as it had been during the previous three years. Thus, for example, the volume of Chinese criticism of the Soviet Union was significantly reduced for four months following Mao's death. Peking did not formally reject the Soviet gestures toward China until mid-November 1976. And, for several weeks following Ilichev's return to Peking, Chinese comment was inexplicably moderate toward the Soviet Union. At the turn of the year, however, Chinese spokesmen once again reaffirmed a firm line against Moscow and the volume of anti-Soviet polemics began to increase noticeably.

The Chinese did not publicize their prompt rejection of Brezhnev's two messages to the Chinese leaders. Their first official response to the Soviet gestures came in a 15 November 1976 speech by Vice Premier Li Hsien-nien at a banquet for a visiting African president. Li accused Moscow of creating "false impressions" of relaxation in Sino-Soviet relations in order to "confuse" world opinion. He maintained that Moscow was engaging in "wishful thinking and day dreaming" about Sino-Soviet reconciliation.

Following Ilichev's return to Peking on 28 November, Chinese spokesmen were moderate in criticizing the Soviet Union until Li Hsien-nien blasted the Soviets as "the main source" of a new world war during a 21 December speech in

Peking. Hua Kuo-feng used a 25 December speech at an agricultural conference in Peking to echo Li's attack of the previous month. He claimed that Moscow was "dreaming" if it hoped for a Sino-Soviet reconciliation. This was followed by Peking's first authoritative criticism of the Soviet position in the negotiations over the border problem in two years. An authoritative 11 January 1977 *People's Daily* article echoed past Chinese complaints that the talks remained deadlocked because Moscow refused to withdraw its troops from disputed border regions. Subsequently, Chinese propaganda stepped up attacks on a broad range of Soviet policies.

Sino-U.S. Relations

The Sino-U.S. reconciliation had its official beginning with President Nixon's 21-28 February 1972 visit to China. The visit was important to China for several reasons: it marked the end of U.S. containment of China and all but eliminated Chinese concern over U.S. forces stationed in Asia. It reflected a reduction in U.S. support for the Taipei government, providing greater leverage and new opportunities for Peking in its continuing effort to gain control of Taiwan. It also enhanced Peking's rising international stature and established a set of Sino-U.S. principles that would govern future developments in East Asia.

The two sides' agreement in their joint communiqué on the need for cooperation in building a new order in East Asia was a significant step for Peking in its efforts to counterbalance its main enemy, the USSR. The communiqué specified that the two sides disavowed any intention to seek "hegemony" in East Asia and opposed any effort by any other country to seek hegemony there. They also pledged not to "collude" with another country against the interests of a third.

Over the next two years, relations developed smoothly as the United States pulled back from forward positions in East Asia, notably from Indochina. Sino-U.S. contacts increased significantly, and were highlighted by the February 1973 agreement to establish Sino-U.S. diplomatic liaison offices. Peking media comment treated the United States more favorably than in the past, and critical reportage on U.S. internal problems was markedly reduced. Thus, for example, even though Peking media in the past had repeatedly and shrilly attacked the United States over American domestic problems, Chinese comment on such issues sharply declined after Nixon's 1972 visit. Chinese treatment of the U.S. domestic scene became generally confined to one or two reports a week on U.S. economic and social problems such as inflation, unemployment, and the plight of minorities. For the most part, such reports were brief and contained little or no critical comment. Chinese comment almost never referred to U.S. internal political developments.

An increase in the number and virulence of critical Chinese reports on U.S. domestic problems came in 1974, coincident with the upsurge in Chinese revolutionary fervor during the massive political campaign to criticize Confucius and Lin Piao. Chinese reportage was more explicit in condemning the "rotten capitalist system" in the United States and the West. Peking media also entered into a new area by criticizing aspects of popular U.S. culture for the first time since 1972. A 27 July 1974 NCNA report—widely broadcast by Peking radio and published in *People's Daily*—hailed the American peoples' resistance to the "decadent culture" fostered by the U.S. "ruling class," which NCNA said aimed to "poison the peoples' souls" with displays of sex and violence on television and in movies and magazines. The impact of the Chinese campaign on coverage of U.S. events was graphically illustrated by another 27 July 1974

NCNA report praising popular resistance in San Jose, California, to the display there of a statue of Confucius which had been brought from Taiwan.

The leftist fostered anti-Confucius campaign also served to complicate the smooth development of Sino-U.S. relations in other ways. Thus, the campaign featured harsh attacks against Western music, films, and other cultural works which served to dampen Chinese interest in cultural exchange with the United States. It prompted harsh criticism of foreign trade with capitalist countries, reducing China's heretofore active interest in commerce with the United States. The campaign also prompted a PRC protest against the presence of U.S. military guards at the U.S. liaison office in Peking, resulting in the quick recall of the guards by the United States. And during the anti-Confucius campaign, Peking took an unusually hard line on the Taiwan issue, giving atypical stress to Peking's determination to strike militarily across the Taiwan Straits in order to liberate Taiwan by force.

As the anti-Confucius campaign subsided in late 1974, the Chinese approach toward the United States was influenced by factors affecting U.S. strategic power in world politics. In particular, three major events coincided at this time to cause serious Chinese concern over the U.S. strength.

1. Although Chinese media never commented on the Watergate scandal, Peking spokesmen made clear in private talks with Westerners—reported in the Western press—that Chinese leaders were concerned that the United States might be entering a period of "isolation" in foreign affairs as a result of its preoccupation with internal problems.

2. The 1974-1975 economic recession had a seriously weakening effect on the United States, according to PRC estimates. An outpouring of Chinese media reports repeatedly depicted the recession as the worst U.S. economic crisis since the 1930s and a vivid reflection of the "weaknesses" of

the Western economic system.

3. The April 1975 collapse of U.S.-backed regimes in Indochina caused the Chinese to question U.S. ability and determination to defend its interests in world affairs.

The Chinese were not satisfied that the Ford administration was following policies which would adequately restore U.S. credibility as a great world power. In fact, the Chinese registered serious reservations over the Ford administration's willingness to compromise with the USSR during the Ford-Brezhnev summit at Vladivostok in November 1974 and during the European security summit conference in August 1975. Chinese concern over the Ford's administration's pursuit of U.S.-Soviet détente was heightened as a result of the president's firing of Defense Secretary Schlesinger in late 1975. Peking spokesmen voiced their concern during the late-1975 visits to Peking by Secretary Kissinger and President Ford.

Peking treatment of Secretary Kissinger during his visit to the PRC in October 1975 was highlighted by a "friendly" meeting with Mao on the 21st. Prior to the meeting, the Kissinger party's visit occasioned correct Chinese protocol treatment, but Foreign Minister Chiao Kuan-hua's remarks at the usual welcoming banquet contained some indirect criticism of U.S. détente policy.

As in the past, Kissinger was welcomed at the airport by a Chinese delegation led by Chiao Kuan-hua, and Vice Premier Teng Hsiao-ping attended the welcoming banquet on 19 October. NCNA reported that Teng and Chiao held talks with Kissinger on the 20th and 21st. NCNA's report of the meeting with Mao duplicated the agency's report of Kissinger's last session with Mao on 12 November 1973 in noting the "friendly" atmosphere and pointing out that the chairman asked Kissinger "to convey his regards" to the president.

Chiao Kuan-hua's toast at the welcoming banquet, as

transmitted by NCNA, departed from past practice in omitting introductory words of welcome for the secretary. Chiao also launched a Chinese warning—not seen before during a Kissinger visit—that détente was an "illusion" that should not blind the world to Soviet expansionism.

Chiao's toast was similar to Chinese welcoming remarks in the past when it observed that "on the whole, Sino-U.S. relations have moved forward in the last few years," and that while there are differences, the two sides "have common points as well." Chiao recalled that "a new page" was turned in relations between the two countries with President Nixon's 1972 visit to China and the issuance of the Shanghai communiqué. But, possibly reflecting less regard for the Ford administration, Chiao made no mention at all of President Ford.

Chinese media treatment of President Ford and his party during their December 1975 visit generally adhered to the strict protocol pattern followed during Nixon's 1972 visit. The U.S. delegation's "friendly" meeting with Mao on 2 December, as well as initial Chinese comment welcoming the visitors, underlined the measured improvement in Sino-U.S. relations that had taken place over the previous three years. However, Chinese comment softpedaled the need for formal normalization of bilateral relations and stressed instead that Peking was concerned over U.S. détente with the USSR. Vice Premier Teng Hsiao-ping on 1 December indicated, in the most explicit terms to date, that China saw a stronger U.S. strategic resolve against the Soviet Union as the most important contribution the Ford administration could make to enhance the Sino-American rapprochement.

Teng Hsiao-ping's remarks at the 1 December banquet echoed stock Chinese assessments of Sino-U.S. bilateral relations which had been set forth most recently in Chiao

Kuan-hua's remarks welcoming Kissinger in October. Teng asserted that "on the whole" relations had improved, and he praised Nixon's 1972 visit and the resulting Shanghai communiqué, calling the latter a "unique international document" which underlines both the "fundamental differences" and the "many points in common" held by our two sides. Teng expressed Peking's "welcome" to President Ford's past affirmations that the United States would abide by the communiqué and seek to improve Sino-U.S. relations, and he voiced routine confidence that relations would be normalized "eventually" through both sides' "joint efforts."

By contrast, Teng devoted unusual stress to "a more important question" involving the need for U.S. vigilance against Soviet international expansion. Though not explicitly mentioning the USSR, Teng harshly attacked "the country which most zealously preaches peace" as "the most dangerous source of war," and he added that "the crucial point is what line or policy" the United States and China would pursue in the face of this mutual threat. Teng exhorted the United States to follow Peking's example, not to fear such "hegemonism," but to form a broad international front against it and to wage a "tit-for-tat struggle." He added that the USSR was "weak by nature" and "bullies the soft" but "fears the tough." Teng underlined the common U.S.-Chinese cause against Moscow by highlighting as "an outstanding common point" the Shanghai communiqué's call for opposition to international "hegemony."

In early 1976, the Chinese made concerted efforts to reassure the United States over Chinese interest in improved relations. This stemmed in part from Peking's desire to show that China's December 1975 démarche toward the Soviet Union—the return of the Soviet helicopter and crew that had been held in China since March 1974—had not affected China's efforts to foster better ties with the United States.

Peking also endeavored to reassure Washington that Chou En-lai's death on 8 January 1976 would not result in a change in Chinese foreign policy.

In the wake of China's unexpected release of the Soviet helicopter crew on 27 December 1975, Peking media treated U.S. visitors to China with rare warmth and softened past criticism of US. policies. Julie and David Eisenhower were accorded an extraordinarily warm and widely publicized welcome during a 29 December-2 January stay which included a visit with Mao; and media reports on a U.S. congressional delegation touring Peking from 30 December-4 January were warmer than those describing previous visits by U.S. congressmen. At the same time, extensive Chinese year-end comment reviewing international developments in 1975 dropped the previous year's more evenhanded criticism of both superpowers to focus attacks on the USSR while markedly softpedaling criticism of the United States.

The Eisenhowers were greeted on arrival on 29 December 1975 by Chinese officials led by PRC Liaison Office Chief Huang Chen, were feted at a banquet hosted by Huang that evening, met with Foreign Minister Chiao Kuan-hua the next day, and had an audience with Mao on the 31st. NCNA said that the meeting with Mao took place in a "cordial and friendly" atmosphere, and it noted that Mao had responded to Julie Eisenhower's conveyance of her father's regards to the chairman with an invitation to former president Nixon to make another visit to China. NCNA reported the next day that a picture of Mao greeting the Eisenhowers was given front-page prominence in the *People's Daily* and all other Peking papers on that day. A later NCNA report on the 1st noted that Vice Premier Teng Hsiao-ping had a "friendly" conversation with the Eisenhowers and hosted a luncheon for them on 1 January 1976.

Following the pattern of previous U.S. congressional

visits to China, the congressional visitors, led by Representatives Heckler and Mink, capped their stay in Peking with separate meetings with Chiao Kuan-hua and Teng Hsiao-ping. Unlike NCNA reports on previous visits, however, the NCNA account of their 2 January meeting with Teng took note of the atmosphere of the occasion, describing it as "friendly." NCNA on 3 January reported the U.S. delegation's reciprocal banquet for their Chinese hosts that day. During visits of previous congressional delegations, the NCNA had failed to report the congressmen's entertainment of their hosts.

Peking's softer line on U.S. foreign policy was apparent in lengthy NCNA year-end commentaries which refrained from treating the United States as a significant international danger while reviewing developments in 1975 in such areas as East Asia, the Middle East, Africa, South America, and the Caribbean. While similar NCNA reviews in 1974 had portrayed the United States as the main danger to third world countries in Latin America, and had voiced evenhanded criticism of both superpowers in Asia, the Middle East, and Africa, this time Peking played up the USSR as the principal menace in all these regions and substantially reduced criticism of the United States. Perhaps the most remarkable example of China's discretion was provided by NCNA's reviews of Asian developments during the previous year. These avoided explicit mention of the U.S. setbacks in Indochina or Asian pressure to remove U.S. bases from Thailand, the Philippines, and Korea, whereas the previous year anti-U.S. developments in Asia had been prominently featured.

After the death of Chou En-lai, Peking used the occasion of Nixon's second visit to China to stress the importance of Sino-U.S. rapprochement. The key tenets of Peking's moderate foreign policy were reaffirmed by China's new acting

premier, Hua Kuo-feng, making his major diplomatic debut
as host to Nixon during the visit that began on 21 February
1976. The Chinese leadership's commitment to improve
Sino-U.S. relations was underlined both by the cordial
reception given the former president and Hua's remarks at a
welcoming banquet on the 22nd. Hua's banquet statements
included a call for greater vigilance against Soviet "expansionism," a theme which had likewise been pressed by
Chinese spokesmen during President Ford's visit to China
the previous December.

Chinese protocol treatment and media coverage of Nixon's visit generally followed the pattern employed during
Nixon and Ford's previous visits. The fact that this visit had
a less official character was reflected, however, in the Chinese
omission of references to some of the ceremonial trappings
surrounding the previous visits by U.S. chiefs of state. Thus,
there were no descriptions of U.S. and Chinese flags being
displayed or references to the playing of the national an-
thems of the two countries, and there was no honor guard to
welcome the former president at the airport.

Hua Kuo-feng led Chinese officials welcoming Nixon at
the airport on 21 February. On the following day the former
president held talks with Hua and paid a condolence visit to
Chou En-lai's widow. On the evening of the 22d he was
hosted at a banquet by Hua and the two exchanged "toasts."
Nixon, accompanied by Hua and other Chinese officials,
met with Mao on the 23rd for a "friendly conversation . . . . on
a wide range of subjects." NCNA's report on the meeting
with Mao included a gesture to the Ford administration,
noting that Mao had asked Nixon to convey his regards to
President Ford. Nixon also held talks with Hua on the 23rd
and 24th, and on the evening of the 23rd he attended a soiree
in the company of Hua and Chiang Ching.

Hua Kuo-feng's strong affirmation at the 22 February

banquet of the importance of Sino-U.S. rapprochement may have been calculated to allay concern that the emerging campaign against Vice Premier Teng Hsiao-ping might jeopardize the Sino-U.S. relationship. Hua echoed remarks by Teng during a banquet for Ford the previous December when he restated Chinese support for the Shanghai communiqué, maintained that there was common ground between the two countries, and recalled Nixon's role in opening relations with China—adding that Nixon took this "courageous action" in his "far-sightedness." Hua went on to implicitly link Mao personally with this policy towards the United States, stating: "The Chinese Government has always pursued and will consistently pursue the line, principles, and policies laid down by Chairman Mao in the field of foreign affairs. We remain convinced that so long as both sides earnestly implement the principles of the Shanghai communique, Sino-U.S. relations will further improve."

Following the death of Mao Tse-tung in September and the arrests of the four leftist Chinese Politburo members the following month, newly installed CCP chairman Hua Kuo-feng took the lead in reaffirming Chinese interest in the United States. Chinese media coverage also reflected a rejection of policies of the gang of four earlier in the year which had prompted a harder PRC line on Taiwan and on trade with the United States. Chinese propaganda was now consistently moderate and restrained in treating the United States.

The *People's Daily* as well as the NCNA highlighted Peking's cordial welcome for an unusually large number of U.S. visitors to China in late 1976. In October, Peking media reported that PRC officials led by Vice Premier Li Hsien-nien held "friendly" talks with a U.S. congressional delegation led by Senator Mansfield, noted Foreign Trade Minister Li Chiang's "friendly" meeting with a U.S. trade delegation, and recounted the enthusiastic Chinese welcome for a U.S. volleyball team touring China. In November Peking media noted the activites of a U.S. congressional delegation led by Senator Curtis and reported the warm welcome by PLA Deputy Chief of Staff Wu Hsiu-chuan for visiting *New York Times* correspondent Drew Middleton. NCNA on 17 November also commented in unusually warm terms on the October tour of the United States by a Chinese volleyball team, observing that the team had seen first hand that "the American people are very friendly to China."

Chinese propaganda on the Taiwan issue remained low-key. At the same time, Peking media took pains to emphasize increased interest in trade with the United States and other capitalist countries—a policy which the leftists had opposed.

Peking propaganda was restrained in its treatment of U.S. government policies. Chinese media sharply reduced attacks on alleged U.S. efforts to "appease" the Soviet Union under the cover of East-West détente. Typically, the main criticism was aimed at the Soviet Union. Thus, for example, an 18 November speech by a Chinese delegate at a UN committee meeting on the Middle East briefly criticized U.S. support for Israel but went on to scathingly denounce the Soviet Union as "more insidious and cunning." Peking did criticize the U.S. veto of Vietnam's application for UN membership, but the criticism was couched in mild terms that went no further than expressions of Chinese "regret" over the U.S. action.

Consistent with its reluctance in recent years to comment on changes in the U.S. administration, Peking made only passing references to President-elect Carter in 1976. A terse 3 November NCNA report noted his election and an equally brief NCNA report on 23 December recounted his cabinet appointments. Peking's only other mentions of Carter that year came in NCNA items on 12 November and 10 December.

The November report noting that a U.S. "Committee on the Present Danger"—formed by former U.S. government officials who were suspicious of Soviet intentions—had urged Carter to increase U.S. defense spending. The item on 10 December reported on the NATO foreign ministers meeting in Brussels and noted, with obvious approval, that Carter had sent a message to the session affirming his commitment to the Atlantic alliance.

Taiwan

China's recent policy on the sensitive issue of Taiwan has been closely intertwined with the development of Sino-U.S. relations. The first indication of Chinese moderation and flexibility on the issue of Taiwan came in the wake of the Sino-U.S. reconciliation in 1972, when Peking media abandoned their longstanding hard line against the Nationalist government in Taipei and its foreign supporters. Following Nixon's February 1972 visit to Peking, and other Chinese diplomatic successes, Peking began to encourage publicly "people-to-people" contacts with Taiwan, sharply reduced criticism of Chiang Kai-shek and other Nationalist leaders, and—for the first time since the mid-1950s—called for peace talks with the Nationalists and the "peaceful" liberation of Taiwan. At the same time, there was a sharp reduction in Chinese media criticism of alleged foreign "schemes" to promote "two Chinas" and keep Taiwan free of Peking's control.

China's approach hardened in 1974 following Taipei's rejection of repeated PRC overtures and a general stiffening in Peking's foreign policy line during the massive Chinese ideological campaign to criticize Confucius. Chiang Kai-shek and other Nationalist leaders were once again severely criticized in Chinese propaganda. Peking stopped calling for the peaceful liberation of Taiwan and stressed instead

China's willingness to use military force to liberate the island. While maintaining circumspection toward U.S. policies, Chinese media renewed harsh criticism of alleged Soviet and Japanese efforts to block Peking's control of Taiwan.

Chou En-lai's 13 January 1975 report to the NPC signaled the start of a more moderate phase in Peking's public approach to Taiwan. Chou emphasized Peking's confidence that "fellow countrymen" in Taiwan would play a major role in what was now seen as a long-term struggle to liberate the island. At the same time, Chinese propaganda began to play down the PLA's possible role in Taiwan's liberation. Peking's new stress on encouraging liberation from within received added impetus following the death of Chiang Kai-shek in April 1975, when Peking propaganda argued that the new regime of Premier Chiang Ching-kuo was far weaker and urged that the people on Taiwan intensify their struggle against the "tottering clique."

Peking's conciliatory overtures were featured in 1972-1973. During the early 1970s, a steady succession of agreements extending recognition to the PRC rapidly eroded the international position of the Republic of China and prompted growing confidence in Peking about international support for its claim to Taiwan. Chinese propaganda maintained that developments such as the October 1971 UN General Assembly vote admitting the PRC into the United Nations, Nixon's February 1972 visit to China, and the normalization of Sino-Japanese relations during former Japanese prime minister Tanaka's September 1972 visit had delivered a "hammer blow" to those trying to block Taiwan's reunion with the mainland. In this new situation, Peking halted its previously routine media charges that the United States, the Soviet Union, Japan, and other countries were trying to keep Taiwan from PRC control. At the same time, attempting to capitalize on its improved international prestige and Taipei's isolation and disarray, Peking undertook a series of gestures designed to overcome traditional ROC distrust of the mainland government and prepare the ground for a major PRC initiative—a proposal for peace talks with Taipei, put forth in February 1973.

Peking's new policy toward the Nationalist regime prompted Chinese media to halt abusive personal attacks on Chiang Kai-shek and to revive favorable comment about Sun Yat-sen, after a hiatus of several years. During a 1 October PRC National Day reception in Peking in 1972, Politburo member Yeh Chien-ying extended a highly unusual invitation to "Taiwan compatriots" to tour the mainland and visit relatives. Stressing sentiments of patriotism among Chinese on both sides of the Taiwan Straits, Yeh declared that all Chinese patriots belong to "one big family" and that no distinction would be drawn between "those who come forward first and those later." He assured Taipei officials that even "those with wrongdoings in the past" were welcome to join the patriotic family.

Peking's official proposal of peace talks with the Nationalists came in a speech by former Kuomintang general Fu Tso-i at a 28 February 1973 meeting in Peking commemorating the 1947 Taiwan uprising against Nationalist rule. Addressing a "few words to the military and administrative personnel" on Taiwan, Fu claimed that Peking's recent diplomatic successes and Taipei's isolation demonstrated that Taiwan's unification with the mainland was the "trend of the times" which "no force whatever can obstruct or undermine." He warned Taipei leaders that they should no longer cherish "illusions" about support from the United States or other powers, claiming that the United States recognized one China and would oppose any effort by Taipei to seek support elsewhere. Stressing that "this situation

cannot be changed," Fu called for talks: "We are all Chinese.
Why couldn't we talk for the sake of the sacred cause of
unifying the motherland?" Citing the example of Mao's
negotiations with Chiang Kai-shek in Chungking during
1945, Fu said that the two sides should come together and
talk, "the sooner the better." He did not mention PRC
preconditions for the negotiations, claiming that Peking
was willing to have either formal or informal discussions,
and promised that China would keep the talks secret if so
desired by the Nationalists. (Peking had not raised the
possibility of peace talks with the Nationalists since the
1950s. A 30 January 1956 report by Chou En-lai to the
Chinese People's Political Consultative Conference had
called on Nationalist officials to negotiate with the PRC in
order to bring about the "peaceful liberation" of Taiwan.)

The possibility of peace talks was not raised in subsequent
PRC public statements,but the concept of "peaceful" liberation of Taiwan did appear in scattered low-level media
comment over the next year. While it was never authorita-
tively endorsed by PRC leaders, Taiwan's peaceful liberation was alluded to by CCP Politburo member Yeh Chien-
ying on 23 July 1973 when he urged a group of "Chinese
patriots" from Hong Kong and Macao to contribute to the
cause of the "peaceful reunification of the motherland."
Judging by the NCNA account, Yeh did not explicitly
mention Taiwan, but the dispatch noted that the meeting
took place in the "Taiwan hall" of the Great Hall of the
People. Subsequently, low-level Peking radio commentaries
beamed to Taiwan repeatedly called on officials and people
in Taiwan to work for "peaceful reunification" and "peaceful liberation" of the island.

Peking's approach to the Taiwan problem hardened at the
end of 1973. Chinese comment over the next year renewed
harsh criticism of Chiang Kai-shek, revived shrill warnings

of Chinese resolve to block suspected foreign efforts to "interfere" in Taiwan, and pointedly raised the specter of a military liberation of Taiwan. The new line may have been prompted by the failure of Peking's forthcoming overtures to elicit a positive response from Taipei, but it also reflected a general hardening in China's foreign policy during the domestic anti-Confucius campaign.

An article in the February 1974 edition of *Red Flag* launched the first major Chinese attack on Chiang Kai-shek in several years. In keeping with the anti-Confucius campaign, the article attacked Chiang primarily because of his long-standing admiration for the ancient Chinese sage. Subsequent Peking comment began—for the first time since 1971—to use epithets such as "traitor" and "political mummy" to describe Chiang Kai-shek.

Chinese criticism of alleged foreign interference in Taiwan focused on Soviet and Japanese policies; Peking's continuing circumspection about Sino-U.S. relations proscribed attacks on U.S. policies toward Taiwan. A 14 December 1973 NCNA article, for the first time in over a year, harshly condemned Soviet contacts with the Taipei government. NCNA reportage and a 2 February 1974 *People's Daily* article also sharply criticized the Seirankai—a rightwing political group in Japan that was allegedly "incessantly entertaining the ambition of seizing the Chinese territory Taiwan."

Fu Tso-i's keynote speech at the February 1974 anniversary reception in Peking underlined the new militancy in Peking's approach. Whereas Fu had confidently predicted the previous year that the PRC's growing international stature would compel Taipei to agree to peace talks, this time he emphasized that Taiwan's reunion with the mainland would result from Chinese determination and PLA preparedness. He pointedly raised the possibility of forceful liberation of Taiwan by the PLA: noting the army's readiness, he stressed that Peking reserved the right to choose the "means by which we liberate Taiwan," and he raised an ominous "cry of warning" that "the Taiwan Straits are today no longer an obstacle to the liberation of Taiwan."

With the conclusion of the anti-Confucius campaign in late 1974, there was a tapering off in shrill polemics concerning Taiwan. Although subsequent Chinese comment continued to routinely note the PLA's "preparedness" to liberate Taiwan, Peking media did not repeat warnings that the Chinese would strike across the Taiwan Straits. Chinese propaganda stressed instead that Peking anticipated that the people of Taiwan, through their protracted struggle, would overthrow the Nationalist regime and bring about the reunification of Taiwan with the mainland.

Signaling the start of the new Chinese line on Taiwan, Chou En-lai's 13 January 1975 report to the NPC laid special stress on the role of the people of Taiwan. Chou called on "fellow-countrymen in Taiwan" to work together with the people of the whole country in order to bring about Taiwan's liberation. PRC Overseas Chinese affairs expert Liao Cheng-chih underlined Chou's call during an address before the February 1975 Taiwan anniversary celebrations in Peking. Liao avoided Peking's warnings of the previous year on the possible use of PRC military power to liberate Taiwan and praised the "compatriots in Taiwan province" who were struggling against the Chiang Kai-shek regime in order to bring about the liberation of Taiwan. Liao voiced Peking's "firm support" for their struggle and expressed confidence that no "reactionary force whatever can thwart the struggle of the people in Taiwan province to liberate Taiwan and unify the motherland."

Chiang Kai-shek's death in April 1975 prompted an intensification in Peking propaganda encouraging resistance in Taiwan. Chinese comment claimed that increasing dissent and disarray had beset the Nationalist government, and it encouraged Taiwan compatriots to intensify their fight against the new "weakened" regime under Chiang Ching-kuo. Speaking at the February 1976 Taiwan anniversary celebrations, Liao Cheng-chih charged that the Chiang Ching-kuo regime was "unprecedentedly enfeebled and isolated" as a result of acute internal "bickerings and rivalries." He claimed that Taipei is "tottering," noted that the struggle of the people in Taiwan "has been going on wave upon wave with growing momentum," and added that people on the mainland "pin our hopes on the people of Taiwan province" to liberate the island.

Peking also began a new series of gestures toward Taiwan following a hiatus during the anti-Confucius campaign. In 1975, Peking announced the release of almost 300 former Nationalist "war criminals" in March, 144 Nationalist secret agents in September, and 72 former Kuomintang military and political leaders in December, noting in each case that those released would be given PRC aid to return to Taiwan if they wished.

Comment after 1974 occasionally noted alleged foreign interference in Taiwan, but avoided the shrill polemics common during the anti-Confucius campaign. Reflecting Peking's more critical view of U.S. foreign policy over the previous two years, Chinese comment during this period began to criticize the United States, as well as the Soviet Union and Japan, for alleged "schemes" concerning Taiwan—a departure from Peking's almost total silence on U.S. policy toward Taiwan following Nixon's 1972 visit. Thus, in April 1975 Peking issued its first authoritative criticism of U.S. policies toward Taiwan since 1972: a low-level PRC official statement decried U.S. opposition to a PRC entertainment troupe's inclusion of a song about

Taiwan's liberation in its repertory during a planned tour of the United States. A year later, a 21 March 1976 NCNA attack on a statement on Taiwan made in Congress by Senator Goldwater represented the first Chinese criticism of a U.S. official on the Taiwan issue in recent years. The United States was also mildly criticized—in contrast with harsher attacks on the USSR—in Chinese comment attacking the superpowers' alleged efforts to foster a "two Chinas situation" at the July 1976 Olympic games. Japan also came under attack in July when NCNA publicized sharp Japanese domestic criticism of then foreign minister Miyazawa's statements urging the United States to slow its departure from Taiwan.

Peking's coverage of the Taiwan issue appeared unchanged in the wake of Senator Scott's disclosure that Vice Premier Chang Chun-chiao had been particularly uncompromising on the Taiwan question during a 13 July meeting in Peking with a U.S. congressional delegation led by Scott. Peking also maintained its standard silence on developments in the U.S. election campaign, giving no hint of Chinese disapproval of the pledges by President Ford and Governor Carter regarding continued U.S. commitments to Taiwan.

Infrequent Chinese comment on Taiwan after the death of Mao Tse-tung on 9 September continued to follow past practice in stressing the importance of the struggle of the people of Taiwan. A 1 October *People's Daily* article signed by Lin Li-yun, a CCP Central Committee member of Taiwanese origin, was written to honor Mao and reaffirm Chinese determination to liberate Taiwan. The article emphasized Mao's influence in encouraging the struggle of people in Taiwan, and claimed that Taiwan residents had followed Mao's instructions in resisting the Japanese during World War II, revolting against Chiang Kai-shek in 1947, and continuing over the past two decades to make "unremitting efforts for the liberation of Taiwan and the reunification of the motherland." "We are convinced," Lin asserted, that "the people on Taiwan" will eventually achieve liberation and "take the bright socialist road under the guidance of Chairman Mao's revolutionary line."

Southeast Asia

The development of Chinese relations with Southeast Asia during the 1970s represents one of the major success stories in recent Chinese foreign policy. Chinese influence has spread rapidly in the region, especially among the noncommunist states, which in the past had strongly feared PRC intentions. Peking's success has been all the more remarkable since the Chinese have also managed to maintain ties with the small Maoist parties which lead armed insurgencies against the noncommunist governments in the region.

Peking has maintained its traditionally close ties with the communist regimes of Indochina, although China's success here has been less pronounced. The communist government in Cambodia continues to regard Peking as its major foreign backer, but communist Vietnam is now treated with suspicion by China. This stems largely from Hanoi's conquest of South Vietnam. Peking at present sees Hanoi as a potential competitor for influence in the region; and, at the same time, the Chinese regret that Hanoi's new influence was attained at the expense of U.S. power in the region. The Chinese also fear that Vietnam will align more closely with the Soviet Union in order to counter China's influence in Southeast Asia and to gain financial and technical aid with which to build up the ailing Vietnamese economy. This, of course, would lead to an expanded Soviet foothold on China's southern periphery—a development which would not be welcomed by Peking.

In the noncommunist countries of the region, however, the Chinese have relied on a dual-track policy—cultivating normal relations with local governments while continuing to lend muted support to insurgent parties within the same countries. China's initial breakthrough in its revived Southeast Asian diplomacy was the normalization of Sino-Burmese relations during Prime Minister Ne Win's August 1971 visit to China. Peking subsequently established formal diplomatic relations with Malaysia in May 1974, with the Philippines in June 1975, and with Thailand in July 1975. The establishment of such relations did not endanger the Maoist communist parties that are leading armed insurgencies against some of these same Southeast Asian governments. Peking publicly muted its own relationship with the insurgents, while China-based clandestine radios continued to serve as outlets for hardline ideology and propaganda attacks on the local governments.

The spring 1975 communist military victories and the ensuing U.S. military withdrawals in Southeast Asia caused several noncommunist states there to reassess their foreign policies and speed up normalization of relations with China. These developments accelerated the pace of Peking's long-range, "step-by-step" measures to enhance Chinese influence. The focus of Chinese media attention shifted markedly. In the past Peking had sought to extend its influence largely at the expense of the United States, encouraging neighboring states to work against U.S. policy in Indochina and to force a reduction of the U.S. presence. Now, Peking portrayed the Soviet Union as the main strategic danger in the region and promoted good Southeast Asian relations with China, regional solidarity, and a continued U.S. military presence in the area as useful bulwarks against alleged Soviet ambitions.

The Chinese people consistently support the just struggles of all oppressed nations and oppressed peoples.
This is our internationalist duty. We hold, at the same
time, that the social system of a country can only be
chosen and decided by its own people and cannot be
imposed by other countries. Countries with different
social systems can develop state relations on the basis of
the five principles of mutual respect for sovereignty and
territorial intergrity, mutual nonaggression, noninter-
ference in each other's internal affairs, equality and
mutual benefit, and peaceful coexistence.

This passage from Chou En-lai's 28 May 1974 banquet
speech for visiting Prime Minister Razak of Malaysia underscored the two basic tenets in China's dual-track propaganda approach to noncommunist Southeast Asian states
over the past seven years. On the one hand, the Chinese have
maintained support for pro-Peking insurgencies led by
Maoist parties which speak against existing regimes in the
name of "oppressed" peoples in the area. On the other, the
Chinese leaders at the same time have developed a steadily
growing effort to improve and normalize state relations with
Southeast Asian governments on the basis of the five principles of peaceful coexistence.

Since the early 1970s, the Chinese have gradually moderated propaganda support in their own name for the small
and generally ineffective communist-led insurgencies in
Southeast Asia that previously had been the focal point of
Chinese foreign policy there. As China emerged from the
internal chaos and diplomatic isolation caused by the
Cultural Revolution, and as the situation in Southeast Asia
became more fluid as the U.S. military withdrawal accelerated, Peking gradually placed more emphasis on improving
bilateral relations with noncommunist Southeast Asian

governments heretofore alienated from China. Peking opted for a long-term, gradual political and economic strategy designed to reassure neighboring states suspicious of Chinese intentions. They used trade deals, unofficial leadership meetings, and formal political consultations with their noncommunist neighbors in order to cultivate feelings of good will or at least reduced suspicion concerning China.

Part of Peking's efforts to reassure the Southeast Asian states was reflected in a gradual reduction of open and direct propaganda support for Southeast Asian insurgencies, but with continued reliance on three PRC-based clandestine radio stations, broadcasting in the name of the Maoist communist parties of Thailand, Malaysia, and Burma, to carry the major load of propaganda support to the antigovernment insurgencies. Thus, while Peking's own media reduced criticism of Southeast Asian regimes and their support for insurgencies, the clandestine radio stations—the Voice of the People of Thailand (VOPT), the Voice of the People of Burma (VOPB), and the Voice of the Malayan Revolution (VOMR)—have carried a daily fare of antigovernment propaganda advocating popular armed struggle against existing authorities. They also have departed from Peking's own media line in sharply criticizing the foreign and domestic policies of Southeast Asian governments.

As a rule, the Peking media no longer attack Southeast Asian leaders by name. The Chinese have also markedly reduced their former practice of replaying reports from the clandestine stations on insurgent battle successes. Peking's infrequent references to the communist parties and to their clandestine radios occur mainly on ceremonial occasions, such as the commemoration of major anniversaries. Maoist party delegates residing in Peking generally receive little high-level Chinese leadership attention.

In the past, Chinese coverage of the Southeast Asian

insurgencies highlighted the importance of the Maoist strategy of armed struggle in the countryside to surround and ultimately annihilate the enemy in the cities. Recent reportage, however, has in addition acknowledged the volatile situation in Southeast Asian cities by encouraging the development of "mass movements" in urban areas.

While the pace and elements of Peking's dual-track policy toward individual Southeast Asian countries have not changed sharply over the past few years, the Chinese have carefully adjusted their strategy to protect PRC interests in the changing situation in the region as a whole. In the early 1970s the Chinese effort centered on expanding Chinese and allied influence in the area and encouraging rapid U.S. withdrawal. Peking harshly rebuked such states as Thailand for their continued support of U.S. bases used in the Indochina war. It scathingly attacked SEATO, U.S. bilateral defense pacts, and U.S. naval activities in the area. The Chinese expressed sharp criticism and suspicion of regional organizations such as the Association of Southeast Asian Nations (ASEAN), seeing them as thinly disguised fronts engineered by pro-West bourgeois states to block Chinese and other communist expansion.

Peking's concern included suspicion of Malaysia's proposal for a Southeast Asian zone of peace and neutrality, which China viewed as a possible effort to build a Southeast Asian diplomatic order blocking Chinese influence. Peking at the same time was on record as vocally supporting Overseas Chinese rights in the area and attacked local authorities over instances of alleged discrimination against Chineses minorities.

The developing Sino-U.S. rapprochement following Nixon's February 1972 visit to China, the continued U.S. military withdrawals from areas throughout China's periphery in East and Southeast Asia, and growing Chinese concern about allegedly enhanced Soviet ambitions in Asia sharply changed the focus of Peking's strategy in Southeast Asia. The Chinese now saw the Soviet Union as the main danger in the area, and Chinese leaders repeatedly warned visiting Southeast Asian dignitaries that in the wake of the U.S. withdrawal from Indochina, they must guard against "letting the tiger in through the back door while repelling the wolf through the front gates."

Peking comment was replete with charges against Soviet military maneuvers, spying efforts, and economic advances in Southeast Asia. By contrast, the United States was criticized only mildly, and some Chinese reportage even played up favorably U.S. and foreign statements on Washington's resolve to remain in the area and protect it against Soviet advances. Thus, Peking has dropped criticism of SEATO and has treated favorably U.S. defense commitments under terms of the ANZUS pact, while at the same time it scathingly denounced what it regards as the true Soviet intentions behind Moscow's proposed Asian collective security arrangement. A 16 June 1975 Peking domestic service radio commentary on U.S.-Soviet rivalry in the region following the U.S. setbacks in Cambodia and Vietnam noted approvingly that the United States was "reluctant to abandon its interests in this region." The commentary acknowledged Assistant Secretary of State Habib's spring 1975 tour of Southeast Asia, viewing it as evidence of U.S. determination to maintain its position as an "Asian and Pacific country" and to play "its deserved and responsible role for the sake of the interests of the United States and this region." The commentary at the same time portrayed the Soviet Union as the principal menace to Southeast Asian independence, trying hard "to replace the United States and dominate Asia."

Peking's altered goals also brought about a shift in the Chinese line on ASEAN. Peking now depicted it as a useful framework for regional stability that would help free the region of big-power influence, particularly that of the Soviet Union. The Chinese media reported regularly on periodic ASEAN meetings, favorably noting progress of the member countries toward regional political and economic cooperation and independence from outside powers. They applauded the ASEAN-backed zone of peace and neutrality in Southeast Asia as a useful means to freeze the USSR out of the region. The Chinese also formally renounced past broad claims to be the protector of Overseas Chinese interests, and for three years Peking media have not been known to have criticized Southeast Asian governments for alleged suppression of Overseas Chinese.

The anti-Soviet emphasis in Chinese regional objectives was pointed up by Peking's efforts to include the so-called antihegemony clause in joint communiqués with Southeast Asian leaders. The clause pledges the signing countries to oppose "any attempt by any country or group of countries to establish hegemony or create spheres of influence in any part of the world." It was included in Chinese communiqués normalizing relations with Malaysia, the Philippines, and Thailand, and was roundly criticized by Moscow as a thinly veiled anti-Soviet PRC scheme in Asia. In the case of the proposed Sino-Japanese treaty, Moscow even formally protested to Tokyo against an inclusion of the clause. Chinese reportage was unusually explicit in underlining Peking's intentions regarding the antihegemony clause. NCNA reports in July 1975 carried comment from the Thai press depicting the use of the clause in the 1 July joint communiqué establishing Sino-Thai relations as a further link in the PRC-fostered "antihegemony front" designed to create the "surest guarantee" for Southeast Asia in the face of "intensified Soviet expansion."

The development of Peking's relations with the various

states in the area has been typified by the course of recent Sino-Malaysian relations. Peking's establishment of formal diplomatic relations with Malaysia in a joint communiqué signed during Prime Minister Razak's May 1974 visit to China was Peking's first such diplomatic breakthrough in Southeast Asia in almost two decades. It set a pattern that was followed in establishing relations with the Philippines and Thailand in 1975. Peking gave a high-level welcome to the Malaysian prime minister that included meetings with Mao and Chou En-lai and it endeavored in the joint communiqué and in Chinese leaders' banquet speeches to reassure the Malaysian visitors about Chinese intentions concerning the pro-Peking insurgency and the large Overseas Chinese population in Malaysia.

Peking media smoothed the way for the visit by dropping past critical references to Malaysian leaders, praising some of Kuala Lumpur's actions in foreign affairs and domestic policy, and reducing customary Chinese media replays of antigovernment news reports from the clandestine VOMR. In line with the persisting Chinese dual-track approach, however, NCNA publicized the 29 April 1975 CCP greetings message marking the Malayan Communist Party's (MCP) forty-fifth anniversary, a step which drew criticism from the Razak government despite the relative mildness of the Chinese message. The CCP's last such publicized message, on the MCP's fortieth anniversary, had extended "warmest fraternal greetings" to the Malayan communists, attacked the Kuala Lumpur leaders by name, and cited Peking's "internationalist duty" to support the insurgents. By contrast, the 1975 message extended only "warm fraternal greetings," avoided reference to Malayan government leaders, and noted only that the CCP and MCP have always supported and encouraged each other; it did not mention any Chinese "duty" to support the MCP. Peking also continued on occasion to refer to the "Communist Party of North Kalimantan," operating at the head of a small insurgency in Eastern Malaysia.

VOMR broadcasts moderated their invective against Razak prior to his China visit, but resumed it soon after his return. VOMR argued, for instance, that Razak undertook the establishment of relations with Peking with ulterior motives, in a vain attempt to ease pressing problems at home and abroad—a notable departure from Chinese leaders' public praise of Razak for coming to China. The clandestine radio has continued to focus on news of guerrilla battle successes and to stress the primacy of Maoist armed struggle, but over the past three years it has given increased attention to urban mass movements in order to capitalize on recent signs of increasing unrest in Malaysian cities. The broadcasts also have stressed the maintenance of MCP unity and orthodoxy and have denounced vaguely defined "splittist tendencies" following a public break of a group of Marxist insurgents from the MCP in the fall of 1974.

Japan and Korea

In two other important East Asian countries—Japan and Korea—the Chinese have adopted approaches far different from those followed in Southeast Asia. In Japan, Peking has focused on consolidating Sino-Japanese relations under terms of a proposed peace treaty which would contain a mutual commitment to oppose "hegemony." Peking's policy toward Korea has been designed to solidify relations with China's close ally in Pyongyang while avoiding any encouragement to the DPRK which might run the risk of a Sino-American confrontation on the peninsula.

Japan

Since the normalization of Sino-Japanese relations during

Prime Minister Tanaka's visit to China in September 1972, progress in bilateral relations has been limited. The main issue blocking progress centers on the conclusion of a Sino-Japanese peace treaty. Peking insists that the treaty must include the antihegemony clause which was contained in the 1972 Sino-Japanese communiqué released at the end of Tanaka's 1972 visit. The treaty would thus serve to round out Peking's use of the antihegemony formula in agreements and communiqués with most other East Asian states, enhancing the utility of this major Chinese diplomatic tool against suspected Soviet expansion in the region. However, Moscow has become increasingly concerned over the antihegemony issue and has repeatedly applied pressure on Japan over the issue. This has caused Tokyo to vacillate over the problem, which has led to a marking of time in Sino-Japanese negotiations on the peace treaty.

While carefully avoiding heavy-handed pressure against Japan, Peking in recent years has used propaganda and diplomatic efforts to encourage Tokyo to sign a peace treaty including the antihegemony clause. Thus, on the one hand, Chinese comment has repeatedly warned the Japanese authorities against "retreating" from the position adopted by Tanaka in the 1972 Sino-Japanese communiqué. On the other hand, it has endeavored to play up anti-Soviet sentiments in Japan, particularly over the sensitive Soviet-Japanese territorial dispute over the "northern territories"— four Japanese-claimed islands north of Hokkaido which have been occupied by the Soviet Union since the end of World War II. In this way, Peking has tried to portray a menace to Japan posed by Soviet "hegemonism" and thereby underline its call for a common Sino-Japanese front.

Peking's approach on the issue was typified by Chinese comment in May 1975 on the occasion of the visit to China of a delegation from the influential Japanese Socialist Party

(JSP). China-Japan Friendship Association President Liao Cheng-chih became the first PRC leader to comment publicly on the treaty issue, during a Peking banquet speech for members of a pro-Peking delegation of the Japanese Socialist Party on 3 May—two days prior to the arrival of the official JSP delegation to China. Liao avoided direct mention of the hegemony issue in a treaty context, but he clearly indicated the PRC position in stating that "we advocate advancing, not retreating from the basis of the 1972 joint communiqué." Liao pledged "joint efforts with our friends in the Socialist party" to have the treaty concluded at an "early date," and NCNA quoted a Japanese speaker at the banquet as saying the JSP delegation had reached "unanimity of opinion" with the Chinese in opposing superpower hegemonism.

At a banquet on 5 May for the official delegation led by JSP Chairman Narita, Liao reiterated as "unswerving" the Chinese demand to "move forward" on the basis of the joint statement. According to the NCNA report on the speech, Liao condemned Soviet "big-power hegemonism" and noted that the Chinese were "willing to join all other people in the world in opposing the hegemonism of the superpowers."

Peking's emphasis on adhering to the joint statement's wording of the hegemony clause was strongly underscored in NCNA's reports on the treaty debate then going on in Japan. A 3 May NCNA item noted that a Japanese Diet member had called the clause an "integral entity," and had said that its two ideas (opposition to hegemony by Japan and China *and* by any other country or group of countries) were "inseparable." The same item cited another Japanese speaker as saying that a treaty without the antihegemony clause would be "not only a retreat from, but also a violation of the joint statement," and that efforts to oppose the treaty were, in fact, efforts to "strangle" the joint statement and undermine the friendship of the two countries.

Soviet Foreign Minister Gromyko's 9-13 January 1976 visit to Japan prompted Chinese polemics typical of Peking's efforts to encourage anti-Soviet sentiments in Japan. Peking observed that the Japanese did not bow to alleged Soviet pressure, especially over the northern territories issue, and it pointedly castigated Gromyko for urging the Japanese not to accede to Chinese wishes nor agree to inclusion of an antihegemony clause in the Sino-Japanese treaty.

Chinese media comment portrayed Gromyko's talks in Tokyo as "heated" and highlighted Tokyo's stand against Moscow on the northern territories issue and against attempts to "inveigle" Japan into the Soviet-proposed Asian collective security system through the "vicious trap" of a Soviet-Japanese friendship treaty. Peking also noted Prime Minister Miki's reported rebuff to Gromyko's warnings about including an antihegemony clause in the proposed Sino-Japanese peace treaty and replayed the prime minister's comments that such a treaty "has nothing to do with the Soviet Union."

A 17 January *People's Daily* article by the prominent anti-Soviet commentator Tung Fang called the northern territories issue the "primary problem" between the Soviet Union and Japan and labeled Gromyko's allusions to the antihegemony clause as "flagrant interference" in Japanese affairs. Tung Fang concluded the article by characterizing the visit as an "ugly performance" which would educate the Japanese people by "negative example." A 14 January NCNA item on the visit further claimed that the visit had shown that the Japanese "did not retreat under Soviet pressure."

The September 1976 defection of a Soviet pilot in a MIG-25 aircraft to Japan led to a serious downturn in Soviet-Japanese relations which Peking was quick to exploit.

Peking played up signs of greater Japanese resistance to the USSR, both over the defection and over such longstanding problems as the northern territories. Thus, for example, a 20 October NCNA dispatch praised the Japanese prime minister's office for marking the twentieth anniversary of Soviet-Japanese relations with advertisements in Japanese newspapers which called for recovery of the northern territories. A 25 October NCNA correspondent's article claimed that Moscow's refusal to exchange messages with the Japanese on the anniversary was merely the latest in a series of alleged heavyhanded Soviet efforts to "pressure" Japan and "pursue a policy of hegemonism." It charged that Moscow had stepped up its pressure in the wake of the MIG incident by canceling scheduled cultural exchanges and trade deals, arresting Japanese fishing near the northern territories, and exerting unspecified "military threats." It also alleged that Gromyko had tried to intimidate the Japanese by "behaving arrogantly" and "loudly rebuking" his Japanese counterpart during a meeting at the United Nations in late September. A 19 October *People's Daily* commentary predicted that Moscow's efforts "will not cow" the Japanese people, who have "risen in resistance" and have entered "the historical epoch of the great struggle against Soviet hegemonism."

Korea

The North Korean government, which has become increasingly disenchanted with Moscow's compromising approach to the United States on a series of international issues, has come to view China as its major international backer. Peking has worked diligently to solidify relations with Pyongyang, but has done so without compromising China's fundamental interest in avoiding a conflict with the United States in East Asia, especially over the sensitive issue of the U.S. troop presence in South Korea. Thus, Peking has given total support for North Korea in its efforts to achieve a "peaceful reunification" of Korea, but has softpedaled statements of support for DPRK actions and pronouncements which might lead to military confrontation with the United States.

China's carefully measured policy was put to the test when DPRK President Kim Il-sung visited China in April 1975—a visit coinciding with the collapse of the U.S.-supported regimes in Indochina. Kim used the occasion to make statements about the United States in Korea and Asia which were widely interpreted in the West as calls for a more militant Asian communist effort against the United States. In contrast, Peking spokesmen used the visit to underline Sino-Korean solidarity, but carefully avoided seconding Kim's allusions to a more militant Asian communist stance.

Peking provided a warm, high-level welcome to the North Korean party-government delegation led by Kim (on his first visit to China since 1961). The cordial reception included a massive welcome at the Peking railroad station and an audience the day of his arrival, 18 April, with Chairman Mao, with whom Kim had a "very cordial and friendly conversation." Following Kim's audience with Mao, his delegation was feted at the customary banquet that evening during which both he and Vice Premier Teng Hsiao-ping spoke. The visit was hailed in a *People's Daily* editorial on the 18th and in Pyongyang's *Nodong Sinmun* on the 20th. On the 19th Kim met with Premier Chou En-lai in the hospital, and began a round of talks with Teng characterized by NCNA as having taken place in a "warm atmosphere of revolutionary friendship and militant unity." On the 22nd Kim and his party left Peking in the company of Teng and Foreign Minister Chiao Kuan-hua for Nanking and a tour of the provinces.

At the welcoming banquet in Peking on the 18th, Kim

observed that this was his first visit "for a long time" and he expressed appreciation for the invitation to come. His delegation, said Kim, would exchange views with the Chinese on present international relations and would "take effective measures for our two people's future common struggle to cope with the fast-changing situation."

Later in the speech Kim spoke of the steady defeats of the "U.S. imperialists" in Asia—passages which were interpreted in the West as indications of Kim's desire for a more militant stance against the "weakened" United States. Observing that the United States had recently been "dealt fatal blows" and was sliding into an "inextricable quagmire of ruin in Indochina," he cited the "great victory" in Cambodia and the virtual collapse of the Saigon regime. Kim drew no direct link between these developments and the U.S. position in Korea, but he significantly characterized the Korean struggle as a "major link" in the chain of the "anti-imperialist national liberation struggle."

Kim summed up the DPRK's policy toward the South when he said: "If U.S. troops pull out of South Korea and a democratic figure with national conscience comes to power in South Korea as its people demand, we will firmly guarantee a durable peace in Korea and successfully solve the question of Korea's reunification . . . by peaceful means." Kim also stated that the North, "as one and the same nation" would not look on with "folded arms" but would "strongly support" the South Korean people should they revolt against South Korean President Park. Kim claimed that peace or war in Korea depended on the United States, "which holds all powers in South Korea." Kim warned that in any future war the North would destroy the aggressors and "only lose the military demarcation line" while gaining the country's reunification.

In discussing the worldwide struggle between imperialist

and the antiimperialist forces, Kim noted the North would be vigilant and "firmly prepared to meet the forthcoming great revolutionary event victoriously, whether there will be war or revolution." (This ominous reference to the "forthcoming great revolutionary event" was in the context of a global struggle and not explicitly linked to the Korean situation.) In discussing North Korean-Chinese unity, Kim asserted that the two countries' destinies were "inseparably linked," a characterization also later expressed in a 20 April *Nodong Sinmun* editorial and in a banquet speech on the 22nd in Nanking by DPRK Vice President Kim Tong-kyu. Kim's speech on the 18th contained the standard North Korean reference to the "blood-sealed" bond between Korea and China, and routinely noted the Chinese volunteers' assistance in the Korean War.

In his banquet speech on the 18th, Teng Hsiao-ping characterized Kim's visit as a "major event of historic significance" in Sino-Korean relations and noted Mao's meeting with Kim earlier the same day. Teng praised the DPRK for its opposition to imperialism and "modern revisionism," one of several standard anti-Soviet barbs in Teng's speech.

Discussing the Korean situation, Teng noted that the DPRK "has repeatedly put forward correct propositions and reasonable proposals for the peaceful reunification of the fatherland." He called attention "in particular" to the three principles incorporated in the 4 July 1972 North-South joint statement, and the five-point program for national reunification put forward by Kim Il-sung on 23 June 1973, noting that they "fully accord with Korea's national interests and enjoy ... extensive international support." Teng accused the "Park Chung-hee clique, supported and instigated by U.S. imperialism," of opposing such proposals and trying to "sabotage" the North-South dialogue.

After lauding the North's attempts at "independent and

peaceful" reunification, Teng went on to say that China has "consistently supported the Korean people in their struggle for the reunification of their fatherland," and he routinely supported "the principles and program advanced by President Kim Il-sung to attain this end."

Addressing the question of the U.S. presence in South Korea, Teng accused the United States of refusing to withdraw its troops and attempting to perpetuate the division of Korea through a "two Koreas policy." He said China "resolutely supported the Korean demand that the United States withdraw all its armed forces from South Korea," but he attached no time frame to such withdrawal.

Teng described "an especially profound revolutionary friendship" between China and Korea, as close as "lips to teeth." However, Teng significantly deemphasized China's past military ties with Korea, failing to repeat Kim's characterization of a "blood-sealed" friendship between the two countries, and he avoided any mention of Chinese participation in the Korean War. Similarly, Teng did not portray the two countries' destinies as "inseparably linked."

The PRC-DPRK communiqué on Kim's visit stressed the complete agreement of both sides on "all questions discussed" and said the visit was "crowned with complete success." The communiqué, carried by both NCNA and the Korean Central News Agency (KCNA) on 28 April 1975, generally did not deviate from well-established North Korean and Chinese policy lines. It took note of the "inspiring" developments in Indochina, but it did not link events there with the situation in Korea. While the communiqué stated a "demand" that the United States immediately stop "aggression and interference" in Indochina, it did not specifically describe events there as a U.S. defeat. Saying PRC-DPRK unity had been "cemented with blood" in protracted struggle against unnamed "common enemies," the communiqué promised that China and Korea would unite "in the common struggle against imperialism and in the cause of socialist revolution."

The Chinese reiterated support for the "peaceful" reunification of Korea and singled out—as had Teng Hsiao-ping's 18 April speech—Kim Il-sung's three principles and five-point proposal as the "correct way" for reunification. Like Teng's speech, the communiqué condemned the "Park Chung-hee clique . . . supported and instigated by U.S. imperialism." Going beyond Teng's speech, the communiqué offered strong—but not unprecedented—support "for the South Korean people of all strata in their just struggle for the democratization of society and the independent and peaceful reunification of the fatherland."

In the communiqué the Chinese condemned "U.S. imperialism" for "attempting to perpetuate the division of Korea" and called for the dissolution of the UN Command and the withdrawal of U.S. troops from the South, but they did not attach any time frame to the demand. The Korean section of the communiqué was brief, containing standard praise of China's domestic political developments and offering support for the liberation of Taiwan.

Sino-Korean solidarity was underlined later in 1975 when a CCP delegation headed by Politburo member Chang Chun-chiao visited the DPRK on 21-27 September—the first high-level Chinese visit to North Korea other than for a major anniversary since Chou En-lai had traveled there in April 1970. The delegation's activities included a 21 September Pyongyang banquet, visits to Kim Il-sung's birthplace and various monuments, mass rallies in Nampo on the 23rd and Pyongynag on the 26th, and a farewell banquet in the capital on the 26th. The delegation was received by Kim on the 24th, and Chang met with Kim again the next day. In his speech at the 26 September banquet, Chang characterized the discussions with Kim as "intimate talks . . . on questions of mutual concern," while the Korean speaker at the banquet, Politburo Committee member Yang Hyong-sop, called them "friendly talks of weighty importance." There were no reports of any other formal talks, although Yang also referred to "comradely and friendly" talks between the CCP delegation and Korean Workers' Party (KWP) members at which there was a "complete consensus of views" on "questions of common concern."

In his several speeches during the visit, Chang stayed within the parameters of Peking's standard line on the Korean issue, but seemed to adopt somewhat tougher language as the visit progressed. At the 21 September banquet he supported Kim's three principles and five-point program as the correct path for Korean reunification, condemned the United States and the Park Chung-hee regime for attempting to perpetuate the division of Korea, and supported the DPRK demand for "complete withdrawal of U.S. troops from South Korea." At a rally on the 23rd in Nampo he included a demand that the UN Command be dissolved. Finally, at the Pyongyang rally on the 26th, he demanded that "U.S. imperialism must withdraw all its aggressor troops and military equipment" from the South, and expressed Chinese support for the "just struggle of the South Korean people." The KCNA text included—but NCNA excerpts of his speech omitted—Chang's accusations that the United States had increased military aid to the Park regime and that the Park "clique," patronized and instigated by U.S. imperialism," was increasing tension on the peninsula by military provocations against the North.

In several of his speeches Chang included standard anti-Soviet barbs, referring to the "superpowers," "hegemonism," and "modern revisionism." As it had done in recent years KCNA carried what were apparently the full texts of these speeches, including the anti-Soviet references.

South Asia

Peking's policy in South Asia during the 1970s has reflected a largely successful Chinese effort to expand relations in the region and to counteract the heavy Soviet influence there. The 1971 crisis over East Pakistan which led to the Indian-Pakistani war later that year prompted a severe downturn in China's influence in South Asia. India, which had long been hostile to China, aligned more closely with the Soviet Union in the August 1971 Soviet-Indian friendship treaty. Pakistan, which in the past had helped China to check Indian and Soviet influence in South Asia, was split in two. The former eastern wing—Bangladesh—adopted decidedly pro-Indian and pro-Soviet policies. The remainder of the small states in the region were cowed by India's demonstration of power during the war against Pakistan, and were unwilling to help Peking challenge India and its Soviet backers in the region.

Over the next three years, Peking adopted a low posture. Although China did what it could to assist Pakistan, Peking had little alternative but to observe events from the outside, hoping for new opportunities. By 1974 two trends in South Asia promised to provide some new openings for Peking. First, India and Bangladesh eventually saw little utility in maintaining their hostility toward Pakistan, and they began serious efforts toward normalizing relations with the Pakistani government. These moves freed Peking—Pakistan's main ally—to normalize China's relations with New Delhi and Dacca. Second, there were increasing signs that these two seats of government were less than completely satisfied with the large Soviet presence in their countries—a trend Peking tried to exploit.

During 1974 the Chinese began to ease past opposition to Bangladesh and India, but progress in normalizing relations was temporarily halted as a result of India's unexpected detonation of an atomic device and its annexation of the former state of Sikkim. After more than a year's wait, the Chinese began, in early 1976, their most significant series of diplomatic initiatives in South Asia. The initiatives were designed to improve China's relations with all South Asian countries at the expense of Soviet influence in the region.

Peking's limited prospects in South Asia during early 1972 were well demonstrated during the 31 January-2 February 1972 visit of President Bhutto of Pakistan to China. Although Peking afforded Bhutto political support and offered some measure of economic relief during the visit, there was an evident effort on both sides to let the dust settle in South Asia while bolstering Bhutto's position during the postwar period. Bhutto was accorded full honors, being hosted by Chou En-lai and received by Mao. The visiting delegation, which included the commanders of the Pakistani armed services, held talks with Chou, his leading associates Yeh Chien-ying and Li Hsien-nien, and PRC defense and foreign affairs officials. According to the communiqué, the two sides were "fully satisfied" with the results of the talks, which had concerned the Indian-Pakistani conflict "and its aftermath," "major" international issues, and bilateral relations.

Despite the strong military representation in the visiting delegation, the only reference in the communiqué to Chinese assistance was a decision to help the development of Pakistan's economy by converting four outstanding loans into grants and deferring payment on a loan provided in 1970. At a banquet given by Chou on 1 February, Bhutto assured his hosts that Pakistan had no intention of being a liability and burden on the PRC and that the delegation was returning home "completely satisfied" with its visit.

For its part, Peking seemed concerned not to have Pakistan become a political liability in the aftermath of the Indian-Pakistani conflict. While offering generalized expressions of support for Pakistan's defense of "state sovereignty and territorial integrity," the Chinese remained noncommital about future relations. The communiqué registered Bhutto's view that relations between "the two parts of Pakistan" should be established through negotiations between the elected leaders and that other states should not in the meantime take "any precipitate action" that would undermine this objective. According to the communiqué, Chou went no further than to express "his understanding of and respect for the above stand" of Pakistan.

While seeking to cut its losses following the defeat of its ally, Peking sought to capitalize on the opprobrium accrued by India and the Soviet Union for their power play in dismembering Pakistan. The joint communiqué, condemning India's "naked aggression" as a defiance of international law, the UN Charter, and the Bandung principles, called upon "the international community to take serious note of the grave consequences that must ensue for the world order" if a country imposes its will on a neighbor by military force. The communiqué also "noted with gratification that the members of the third world in general and the Islamic countries in particular" had supported Pakistan in defense of its territorial integrity.

Though the Chinese muted their anti-Soviet polemics in deference to Bhutto's interests and concentrated their fire on the Indians during his visit, a 31 January *People's Daily* editorial blistered the Soviets for supporting the dismemberment of Pakistan in the name of national liberation. As for the question of Kashmir, the Chinese joined their visitors in the joint communiqué in calling for withdrawal to positions "which respect the cease-fire line in Jammu and Kashmir"; on 1 February Chou declared Chinese support for "the people of Kashmir in their just struggle for the right to national self-determination." As in the case of a 16 December PRC government's statement on the Indian-Pakistani conflict, the 31 January *People's Daily* editorial pointedly offered a reminder that it is in India that "sharp national contradictions and oppression really exist," citing the "just struggles against national oppression" being waged by the Nagas, Mizos, Sikhs, and other nationalities.

By mid-1974, the agreements between India and Pakistan to implement the 1971 UN resolutions on returning prisoners of war and normalizing relations prompted expressions of greater Chinese interest in improved relations with India and Bangladesh. At the same time, Peking continued to support Pakistan. Bhutto, now prime minister, returned to Peking on 11-14 May 1974 and the Chinese gave him the same full honors shown during his visit in early 1972.

Chinese public statements during Bhutto's visit this time pointed to the need for reconciliation in South Asia, while predictably praising Pakistan's struggle to sustain its sovereignty and independence. Teng Hsiao-ping's banquet speech on 12 May offered formal Chinese approval for the final implementation of the 1971 UN resolutions, stressing that these "new developments" had created "favorable conditions" for normalizing relations among countries on the subcontinent. Focusing on Peking's own intentions, Teng went beyond the usual Chinese affirmation of friendship with the "peoples" of the region, asserting that Peking was now ready to develop relations with the "countries" of the subcontinent on the basis of the five principles of peaceful coexistence.

In marked contrast to Chinese comment during Bhutto's 1972 visit, Chinese spokesmen this time studiously avoided direct criticism of India's policies in South Asia. They instead endeavored to portray China as having a common, antisuperpower interest with South Asian states, stressing that these states should be particularly vigilant against Soviet intentions. An 11 May 1974 *People's Daily* editorial warned that the Soviets were "threatening the security" of the area. Teng's 12 May address, in referring to the 1971 war, placed full blame on the USSR for initiating the conflict while avoiding any mention of India's role. The joint communiqué on the visit did contain indirect criticism of India as well as the Soviet Union, noting the need to maintain vigilance against "tendencies toward hegemonism and expansionism" in South Asia and also stating their opposition to "foreign" interference there. As Chou En-lai had done during Bhutto's previous visit, Teng on 12 May affirmed Chinese support for Kashmiri "self-determination." Peking reiterated this stand in the joint communiqué.

Teng's avowal of PRC interest in improved relations with India was followed by other demonstrations of Chinese interest in normalization. However, the process was compli-cated by China's negative response to India's atomic blast and its annexation of Sikkim. Showing Peking's cautious receptivity to improved relations with India, Yeh Chien-ying on 13 June 1974 told a visiting Indian friendship delegation that "the friendship between the Chinese and Indian peoples has a long history," adding: "We believe that the traditional friendship between the two peoples will surely be further consolidated." NCNA reported that Yeh had a "cordial and friendly" talk with the delegation.

On 3 September 1974, however, a *People's Daily* article under the byline "Commentator" offered an authoritative criticism of India's policy toward Sikkim. It denounced the 29 August 1974 Indian government proposal for a constitu-tional amendment to give Sikkim a status similar to that of an Indian state as a "flagrant act of colonialist expansion," and alleged that reducing Sikkim to an Indian colony was merely part of India's longstanding design to become a "subsuperpower" and to "lord it over South Asia." Making a rare reference to past Indian territorial aggrandizement fostered by Nehru, the article went on to accuse Indira Gandhi's regime of going even further along the expansionist road, citing its use of India's atomic test earlier that year to engage in "nuclear blackmail."

Peking typically charged an alleged supportive Soviet role behind India's moves, asserting that Moscow's backing for increased Indian control over Sikkim had bared its position as "protector of the Indian expansionists." Peking saw the cooperation between the two states as "the main cause" of instability in South Asia and "a serious threat" to other South Asian states.

The Chinese followed up with an 11 September 1974 PRC Foreign Ministry statement which offered (for the first time) explicit Chinese support for Sikkimese resistance to Indian rule. Similar to the commentator article, the statement denounced the Gandhi government by name and linked its incorporation of Sikkim with past Indian dismemberment of Pakistan and alleged Indian designs to use its atomic test to "do whatever it pleased with its neighbors." The statement also echoed charges against Moscow's alleged role in supporting New Delhi's "colonialist moves."

Peking capped its invective with a 29 April 1975 PRC government statement strongly denouncing India's "illegal annexation" of Sikkim. The PRC statement contained elements not found in the 11 September 1974 PRC Foreign Ministry statement, while omitting some of the earlier charges. The new statement declared that "China absolutely does not recognize India's illegal annexation," and it accused New Delhi of indulging in the "fond dream of a great Indian empire" and subjecting its neighbors to twenty years of "control, interference, subversion and bullying." The current statement omitted criticism of India's nuclear power development plans that had been contained in the September 1974 Foreign Ministry statement, as well as the earlier statement's personal reference to Indira Gandhi.

During the next year Peking's suspicions about Indian expansionism in South Asia were markedly reduced as the New Delhi government tried to cope with serious internal crises caused by political scandals surrounding Mrs. Gandhi's leadership and dire economic conditions in India. The August 1975 military coup in Bangladesh was also seen in Peking as a curb to Indian as well as Soviet ambitions. The new Bangladesh leadership dropped the previous regime's stress on good relations with New Delhi and Moscow, and aligned much more closely with Pakistan and conservative Islamic states.

Against this more favorable background, Peking in early 1976 began to embark on its most important series of initiatives in South Asia. The Chinese managed over the next year to consolidate their relations with Pakistan, Sri Lanka, and Nepal—South Asian states traditionally friendly to China. And, at the same time, they gained considerably more influence with Bangladesh, Afghanistan, and India—South Asian states which had long been cool to the PRC.

Peking did not immediately report the April 1976 Sino-Indian agreement to resume bilateral ambassadorial-level relations—relations which had not existed since the early 1960s. However, Chinese media comment and leadership statements clearly underlined a new, positive look in Peking's approach toward New Delhi. The capstone of this effort was a December 1976 visit of an Indian friendship delegation to China. The Indian delegation came to China to attend ceremonies marking the opening of the Dr. Kontis Memorial Hall at the Norman Bethune International Peace

Hospital in Shihchiachuang, Hopei Province. Dr. Kontis was an Indian surgeon who died while assisting the PLA during World War II. According to a lengthy NCNA report of 9 December, the ceremonies were attended by a Chinese leadership delegation headed by top-level Hopei officials and were addressed by the president of the Chinese People's Association for Friendship with Foreign Countries, the head of the Indian delegation, and the Indian ambassador. The speeches repeatedly praised Dr. Kontis as a symbol of past Sino-Indian friendship and a model for future cooperation. Although other speakers limited their testimonials to praise for the friendship between the Chinese and Indian "people," the Indian ambassador, as reported by NCNA, used the occasion to convey the "friendly sentiments" of the Indian "Government" to the PRC "Government."

The Indian visit came against the backdrop of reduced Chinese media criticism of Indian policies and increased propaganda support for Sino-Indian friendship. Thus, for example, the visit of a Chinese friendship delegation to New Delhi during September 1976 was highlighted by a 26 September banquet—reported by NCNA on the 28th—at which Indian officials and the Chinese ambassador portrayed the resumption of Sino-Indian ambassadorial relations as the opening of a "new chapter" in the history of their "friendship." (Peking media did criticize India in a 23 November NCNA commentary which supported Bangladesh and mildly chastised India for the Indian-Bangladesh dispute over the sharing of water from the Ganges River.)

Propaganda suggested that Peking's rapprochement with New Delhi was aimed largely at encouraging India to join other South Asian states in resisting Soviet influence in the area. Thus, Chinese media played up alleged signs of Indian dissatisfaction with Moscow. A 20 July NCNA commentary, for example, claimed that India was unhappy with Soviet economic "exploitation" under the cover of "aid." At the same time, Chinese comment stressed the need for the peaceful settlement of disputes among South Asian states and for the development of closer regional cooperation in order to protect the area from Soviet "ambitions."

Coincident with the new approach toward India, the Chinese launched initiatives toward other states in South Asia. Peking gave Nepalese King Birenda a warm, high-level welcome during his 2-9 June 1976 visit to China's Szechuan Province and Tibet. On 3 September 1976 NCNA announced the conclusion of agreements for three major Chinese aid projects in Afghanistan, and Peking later gave a high-level welcome to an Afghan friendship delegation which arrived in China in October. The friendship delegation was received by Vice Premier Li Hsien-nien and had a "cordial and friendly conversation" with him on 1 November. Peking further solidified its traditionally friendly relations with Pakistan and Sri Lanka by extending cordial receptions to Pakistani Prime Minister Bhutto during his 26-30 May 1976 visit to Peking, and to the head of the Sri Lankan navy during his 5-17 November tour of China.

The highlight of these efforts came during the warm Chinese reception greeting a Bangladesh delegation led by head of government Ziaur Rahman during its 2-5 January 1977 visit to Peking. This first official Bangladesh visit was capped by a meeting with Chairman and Premier Hua Kuo-feng and the conclusion of an agreement on economic aid and trade. The visit underlined a warming trend in PRC-Bangladesh relations that began after Ziaur assumed power during a military coup in August 1975.

Ziaur's arrival in Peking on 2 January was marked by a *People's Daily* editorial and the official delegation which greeted him at the airport was headed by Hua Kuo-feng and Vice Premier Li Hsien-nien. Li hosted and spoke at a welcoming banquet for the visitors that evening and also spoke at a banquet hosted by Ziaur on 4 January. Hua, Li and Ziaur attended the 4 January signing ceremonies of PRC-Bangladesh aid and trade agreements.

Declaring in his banquet speech on the 4th that the Bangladesh visit—"the first contact between leaders of our two countries"—had been a "complete success," Li noted that Hua Kuo-feng had had a "cordial and friendly conversation" with the visitors earlier that day and cited the new PRC-Bangladesh agreements as proof that China would "support and assist" Bangladesh as part of Peking's "bounden internationalist duty."

Chinese spokesmen did not echo Ziaur's 2 January criticism of India for its position in the dispute with Bangladesh concerning sharing of Ganges River water and recent armed border clashes. Thus, Li Hsien-nien's banquet speech on the 2nd went no further than to promise Chinese support for the "struggle" of the Bangladesh people against "foreign interference." Li focused his invective on the Soviet Union, criticizing the Soviets as being "the most dangerous source of a new war" and the main danger to South Asian security, and as harboring a "sinister intention to control and enslave the South Asian countries."

Europe, the Middle East, and Africa

Toward areas of less direct concern to Chinese interests such as Europe, the Middle East, and Africa, Peking has done whatever it can to complicate Soviet interests and block suspected Soviet expansion. Of course, Peking has applauded efforts by local governments to unite against the Soviet's "outside interference." At the same time, Peking has maintained a generally positive view of U.S. involvement in these regions—seeing the United States as making a useful and important contribution in shoring up anti-Soviet positions abroad.

Europe

Continuing its favorable assessments of the U.S. defense commitment to Western Europe and the NATO alliance, Peking took note of the May 1976 NATO foreign ministers meeting in Oslo, Norway. A lengthy report on 23 May focused on statements at the session testifying to Western vigilance and military resolve against the Soviet Union. The report was consistent with the Peking media's portrayal of a growing resistance to détente in public opinion and among leaders in the West, especially following the Soviet involvement in Angola in early 1976. At the same time, however, the NCNA account unusually chided the U.S. administration, and especially Secretary Kissinger, for persisting at that time in a détente policy with Moscow in spite of opposition in the United States and Western Europe. Thus, the current report depicted Kissinger as out of step with his NATO colleagues at the meeting, noting that he supported a strong Western defense but had also attempted "to justify his policy toward the Soviet Union, describing it as 'the only viable course.' " Comment later in the year portrayed the United States as back in line with the allegedly anti-Soviet leanings of its NATO allies.

NCNA's treatment of Kissinger at the May 1976 NATO meeting contrasted with its report on the last such NATO session in December 1975, when it had depicted the secretary as being in the forefront of Western leaders warning against Soviet intentions. The portrayal of Kissinger as a vigilant foe of Moscow previously had been a standard theme in Peking propaganda, but for a period of several months—as in the NCNA report on the May 1976 NATO meeting—Peking had avoided emphasizing his statements of resolve against Moscow and had suggested that U.S. policies under his guidance had mistakenly attempted to "appease" the Soviets. This theme had been pressed, for example, in Peking media reports of spring 1976 that cited Western comment criticizing the "Sonnenfeldt Doctrine" as a paradigm of Kissinger's efforts to respond to Soviet "advances" by means of appeasement.

A "newsletter" from a *People's Daily* reporter, broadcast by Peking to domestic audiences on 22 May 1976, deplored the trend of appeasement it claimed had been evident in the West from the time of the Helsinki European security conference and the appearance of the Sonnenfeldt Doctrine. The reporter likened such attitudes to the appeasement of Hitler in the 1930s. He also deprecated U.S. compromise proposals at the European force reduction talks in Vienna as ill-conceived and—in a thinly veiled allusion to Kissinger— deplored the view of "some people" who held that the Soviet Union could not be prevented from emerging as a superpower and should therefore be encouraged to assume a more moderate foreign policy.

The bulk of the NCNA report cited passages from the final communiqué of the NATO meeting and remarks by leading NATO officials to show that allegedly stepped-up Soviet military preparations since the European security conference summit in Helsinki, and especially Moscow's intervention in Angola, had aroused apprehension and greater vigilance in Western countries. NCNA highlighted the NATO ministers' calls for sustained and increased Western defense spending on both conventional and nuclear forces to cope with the Soviet "threat." It cited their complaints about the continued growth of Warsaw Pact forces and the lack of Soviet willingness to compromise in the European force reduction negotiations, and noted NATO references to wider Soviet aspirations in Angola and Africa.

Peking's continuing encouragement of anti-Soviet resistance in Western Europe showed a new twist in mid-1976 when Peking media for the first time began to portray the independent-minded West European communist parties as impediments to Soviet ambitions in the region. Peking media's first comment on the debate between Moscow and the European communist parties during 1975-1976 on issues of doctrine and authority within the international communist movement applauded the independent parties for resisting Soviet efforts to enforce uniformity. The Chinese position was first set forth in a 29 May 1976 Peking domestic service article signed by the prominent anti-Soviet commentator Hsiao Lou, who charged that the "proletarian internationalism" advocated by Moscow was designed to strengthen Soviet "hegemonism" over communists resisting Soviet control. An NCNA commentary on 6 June denounced Moscow's tactics in more detail, noting specifically that they were aimed at parties in both Eastern and Western Europe. A second Hsiao Lou radio commentary, broadcast on 7 June, alluded to Moscow's special problems with the Italian Communist Party (PCI).

The 29 May article characterized recent Soviet warnings against deviation from internationalism as thinly disguised efforts to wield a "big club" in order to force deviant European communists to "come to terms." The NCNA commentary on 6 June, specifically citing statements by Brezhnev as well as authoritative Soviet press comment on the issue, maintained that Moscow's warnings would have little effect. Claiming that the international communist movement was in an unprecedented state of disarray, NCNA asserted that Moscow's recent "outcry" merely showed that "the new tsars are being deserted by their followers" and that "the revisionist bloc is falling apart," Moscow having been reduced to a state of "helplessness."

Peking did not mention any of the recalcitrant Western

European communist parties by name, but NCNA observed that Moscow's so-called "fraternal parties" in Western Europe were "no longer so docile as before" and have often "sung a tune opposite to that of Moscow and openly refused to let their countries follow the example of the Soviet Union." Implying that Peking still viewed these parties as revisionist, NCNA described their national routes to socialism as "allegedly" conforming to their countries' historical and social conditions.

The 7 June 1976 Hsiao Lou radio commentary similarly avoided naming the Italian Communist Party, even though it clearly alluded to the PCI's problems with Moscow at a time when the party was considering participation in the Italian government. Moscow had recently "flown into a rage," it said, and had warned that if "a certain party in Europe" began to take part in the government, it must "adopt the Soviet experience and follow in Moscow's steps" or it will be accused of "insubordination."

Prior to this spate of comment, Peking had acknowledged Moscow's polemic with independent European parties by publicizing—without comment—excerpts from a 1 April 1976 Romanian article on the issue. The 22 April NCNA account of the article highlighted the Romanian article's rejection of the notion that the Soviet experience constituted a universal model to be followed by all parties, and its refutation of the Soviet view of internationalism. Until then, Peking had not even indirectly taken note of similar dissidence among the Western European parties. Occasional allusion to the West European parties during the previous year had been in a critical vein, portraying them as "pro-Soviet forces" which Moscow would use in order to penetrate West Europe and spread Soviet influence at the expense of the United States.

The Middle East

Peking has seen the Soviet Union as on the defensive in the Middle East ever since the initial Arab-Israeli disengagement accords were negotiated under U.S. auspices in 1974. By late 1976, Peking media reports on Middle East developments portrayed the Soviets as thwarted in attempts to make a comeback in the area following Egypt's abrogation of the Soviet-Egyptian treaty in March 1976. Attributing Soviet reverses to the combined efforts of the United States and the Middle Eastern countries themselves, comment from NCNA and *People's Daily* played up the anti-Soviet implications of the 23-24 June 1976 Arab quadripartite conference in Riyadh, Arab media charges of Moscow involvement in the abortive 2-3 July 1976 coup in Sudan, and decisions by Jordan and Iran to buy more weapons from the United States.

The view that the Soviets were on the defensive in the Middle East had generally prevailed in Peking comment for several years. In early June 1976, however, Chinese media atypically reflected concern that Moscow might be able to regain the offensive and recoup its influence in the face of stalemated U.S. efforts to achieve an Arab-Israeli peace settlement. Subsequently, by emphasizing broad resistance to Soviet policy in the Middle East, Peking propaganda suggested that the Chinese were once again confident that the Soviet Union had few prospects in the region.

A 26 June NCNA commentary praised the Riyadh conference—attended by the prime ministers of Egypt, Syria, Kuwait, and Saudi Arabia—for thwarting Soviet efforts to spread its influence by "sowing discord" between Egypt and Syria. NCNA claimed that Moscow had worked hard to prevent the conference from taking place, and noted that the meeting's successful conclusion dealt a "head-on blow" to Kremlin interests.

A 12 August 1976 NCNA commentary ridiculed Moscow's "clumsy efforts" to capitalize on U.S.-Jordanian differences over the proposed sale of U.S. antiaircraft missiles to Jordan. NCNA noted that Moscow had tried to "squeeze into Jordan" by hurriedly sending a military delegation to Amman to offer Soviet weapons, and said that Soviet officials had courted King Hussein during his 17-28 June 1976 visit to the USSR in order to win approval of the arms deal. Claiming that the Soviets were "cocky with success" following the king's visit, NCNA observed that Jordan's subsequent decision to buy U.S. instead of Soviet weapons came "like a bolt from the blue" and dealt another "head-on blow" to the USSR.

NCNA commentaries on 13 and 25 August and a 31 August 1976 *People's Daily* commentary scoffed at the Soviet media's criticism of the five-year U.S.-Iranian arms deal signed during Secretary Kissinger's 5-8 August visit to Iran. Peking strongly defended Iran's arms purchases as "necessary measures" in the face of the massive "threat" posed by the USSR and applauded Iran for taking the lead in the struggle against "big-power hegemonism" in the Persian Gulf area. *People's Daily* claimed that Moscow was using media criticism to "blackmail" Iran, but predicted that the Shah's government would not be cowed.

Africa

Peking's tacit support for U.S.-backed efforts to block Soviet expansion in Africa was seen in the Chinese media's cautious response to Secretary Kissinger's shuttle diplomacy in Southern Africa in late 1976. Peking's favorable characterization of Kissinger's efforts signaled an end to China's indirect criticism earlier in the year of Kissinger and the U.S. administration for being weak in dealings with the USSR.

Peking acknowledged Kissinger's activities only belatedly

with a terse reference in an NCNA commentary criticizing alleged Soviet interference in the area. The commentary, broadcast on 23 September, reported nothing of the substance of the secretary's 14-22 September mission, mentioning it only in passing as an example of U.S. attempts to counter Soviet "expansionism" in the region. The commentary favorably quoted remarks made by Kissinger before his African tour in spring 1976 on Washington's resolve to deter further Soviet gains in Africa after Angola, and claimed that Moscow was "greatly annoyed" by Kissinger's diplomacy and by the African visits of other high-ranking U.S. officials that summer. Implicitly providing a justification for U.S. diplomatic activity in Southern Africa, the commentary outlined at length the variety and scope of Soviet tactics to bring Africa under its "sphere of influence."

The 23 September commentary contrasted sharply with the evaluation of the secretary's African tour in spring 1976. At that time, an NCNA report dismissed some of the same remarks now quoted favorably as "empty threats" demonstrating U.S. "impotence" in the face of aggressive Soviet expansion in Angola. Peking media first portrayed Washington as effectively meeting Soviet challenges in Africa in a 17 July 1976 NCNA report describing Washington's "energetic diplomatic activities" in Africa to "counterbalance the extensive Soviet military influence" and to safeguard "U.S. and Western strategic and economic interests" in the region. Like the current commentary, the NCNA report claimed that Washington's diplomacy had "infuriated" Moscow.

Peking's failure to criticize Kissinger's negotiations or report the initial reaction of African leaders suggested that China now believed that this new round of diplomacy could be fruitful. The previous spring, by contrast, the NCNA report on Kissinger's Africa tour had criticized his statements supporting majority rule in Rhodesia, self-determination in

Namibia, and an end to South African apartheid as merely
an effort to "steal the Russians' thunder." In reporting
Kissinger's talks with South African Prime Minister Vorster
in June 1976, NCNA had also impugned the secretary's
support for a negotiated end to South African apartheid as
motivated in part by a U.S. desire to "conserve the interests of
the white racists."

Disarmament

Since the detonation of China's atomic bomb in 1964, a
major feature of China's propaganda on disarmament has
been the justification of Peking's development of nuclear
weapons and the discrediting of the partial disarmament
measures of the Soviet Union and the United States. As in the
case of other Chinese foreign policy activity, Chinese initiatives on disarmament were sparse during the Cultural
Revolution. As Peking emerged as a major international
power in the early 1970s, the Chinese stepped up efforts
designed to offset superpower—especially Soviet—disarmament measures. This Chinese policy led to a major debate
between Soviet and Chinese representatives at the United
Nations in 1972. Subsequently, heavy Chinese propaganda
attacks have focused against Moscow's stepped-up détente
policies.

Peking's counter to U.S.-Soviet backed partial disarmament measures has long been a call for the total destruction
of nuclear weapons. Peking's stand was first seen in a PRC
government statement following the first Chinese nuclear
test on 16 October 1964. It proposed that a world summit
conference be held to discuss the complete prohibition and
thorough destruction of nuclear weapons, stipulating that
"as a first step," the conference would reach an agreement to
the effect that the nuclear powers undertake not to use
nuclear weapons against each other or against non-nuclear

countries and nuclear-free zones. The proposal was dispatched to world heads of government in messages from Chou En-lai the day after the Chinese test.

Peking propaganda continued to attack the United States and the Soviet Union for refusing to accept China's proposal and for continuing the nuclear arms race under the cover of partial disarmament measures. Thus, for example, a 4 November 1969 NCNA report harshly criticized the announcement of the start of U.S.-Soviet negotiations in Helsinki on strategic arms, affirming that the negotiations were just another step by each power to maintain nuclear superiority by placing restrictions on the other. The dispatch asserted that since the conclusion of the partial test-ban treaty in 1963, the United States and the USSR had done nothing to relax "their nuclear arms expansion and war preparations," but had in fact intensified the development of nuclear weaponry.

Peking's more active interest in disarmament issues following the hiatus in Chinese foreign affairs during the Cultural Revolution was seen in NCNA's 1 November 1970 report of a joint statement that day of the China-Japan Friendship Association and a visiting Japanese Socialist Party delegation. The statement contained the first reference in Peking propaganda since 1966 to the Chinese proposal for a world summit conference to discuss nuclear disarmament. The proposal had last been noted in authoritative Chinese media in Chou En-lai's 28 July 1966 message to the twelfth Gensuikyo-sponsored world conference in Japan against atomic and hydrogen bombs.

In 1971, Peking responded to a Soviet proposal for a conference of the world's five nuclear powers to discuss nuclear disarmament. Chou Enlai told Western journalists visiting Peking that participation in talks limited to the nuclear powers ran counter to China's policy of shunning big-power politics. Chou indicated that the PRC would continue to insist that the talks be open to all nations. The Chinese formally rejected the Soviet bid in a 30 July 1971 PRC government statement which pressed the Chinese position that all the nations of the world should participate in talks on nuclear disarmament. Reviewing disarmament measures from the 1963 partial test-ban treaty to the strategic arms limitation talks, it observed that none had in any way restricted the nuclear arms race between the United States and the USSR. The peoples of the world, according to the statement, had lost confidence in disarmament talks between the nuclear powers, and they rightly held that it was impossible to settle the question of nuclear disarmament by depending upon the two "nuclear superpowers" or by adding more nuclear powers to the talks.

The statement took the occasion to assert that the PRC—whose weapons are still in the "experimental stage"—would never be "a 'nuclear superpower' practicing the policies of nuclear monopoly, nuclear threats, and nuclear blackmail." It insisted that China was developing nuclear weapons purely for defensive purposes in the face of "imperialist nuclear threats."

The statement repeated the long-standing Chinese proposal for a summit conference of all countries of the world to discuss the complete prohibition and thorough destruction of nuclear weapons and, as a first step, to reach an agreement on nonuse of nuclear weapons. It also reaffirmed the Chinese pledge to seek the complete prohibition and thorough destruction of nuclear weapons and the PRC's commitment not to be the first to use nuclear weapons.

On the non-first-use question, the statement went on to challenge the United States and the USSR, which "possess large quantities of nuclear weapons," to issue statements "separately or jointly to openly undertake the obligation not to be the first to use nuclear weapons at any time or in any circumstances," to dismantle all nuclear bases on the territories of other countries, and to withdraw all nuclear weapons from abroad. Such steps, the statement observed, would be a test of Washington's and Moscow's desire for nuclear disarmament. Although Peking had so challenged the United States before, the challenge to the USSR was new—an indication of the increasingly anti-Soviet thrust in Chinese policy on disarmament.

The anti-Soviet direction of Chinese disarmament policy was made vividly clear at the United Nations in Chinese delegate Chiao Kuan-hua's 26 September 1972 speech before the General Assembly. Chiao responded to Soviet charges accusing the Chinese of trying to "artificially divorce" the problems of conventional and nuclear weapons, which had been contained in a Soviet proposal for an agreement on nonuse of force offered earlier in the session. Chiao placed new emphasis on conventional arms, along with nuclear, in his own disarmament position. Contending that the most urgent question was the withdrawal of foreign forces rather than the reduction of armaments, Chiao added: "Let the two superpowers withdraw all their armed forces, both conventional and nuclear, back to their own countries."

Chiao aimed his remarks on disarmament at the Soviet draft resolution which had coupled the renunciation of the use of force with a permanent ban on the use of nuclear weapons, at Moscow's revived call for a world disarmament conference (WDC), and at the Soviet call for a comprehensive nuclear test ban. Chiao accused the Soviet Union of propounding an "alarmist theory" when it had argued in support of its nonuse of force proposal that the destructive power of even conventional warfare had advanced so greatly that the use of conventional weapons alone could lead to the annihilation of entire nations. He emphasized that the nonuse of force in international relations can only be conditional. He underscored Peking's insistence on the relation between just and unjust wars in concluding that an agreement on nonuse of force should not apply to struggles against imperialist aggression and colonialism, and suggested that a proposal for a ban on aggression in international relations might have been more appropriate.

Chiao reaffirmed the Chinese view of Moscow's concept of a world disarmament conference. Criticizing Gromyko's letter on WDC to UN Secretary General Waldheim on 4 August 1972, Chiao claimed that a WDC without a clear aim would in fact be an "empty talk club" serving only to "hoodwink and lull the world." Listing prerequisites for such a conference, he went beyond his statement of the previous year that nuclear countries must first pledge never to be the first to use nuclear weapons and must dismantle and withdraraw all nuclear forces stationed abroad; now including conventional forces, Chiao stated that the nuclear countries had to withdraw all types of forces from abroad.

Although Chinese spokesmen have continued to sharply attack Soviet disarmament proposals in the United Nations, the bulk of China's effort in this field has focused in recent years on countering Soviet détente and disarmament proposals with the West. The Chinese have taken particular pains over the past three years to attack the Soviet-fostered notion that détente has achieved great advances, and have stressed instead that U.S.-Soviet rivalry has in fact intensified under the cover of the various détente agreements. To counteract Soviet propaganda on détente, Peking even altered its view of the overall international situation. The Chinese began to stress that U.S.-Soviet rivalry had become so intense that the world was bound to experience "a new world war."

Typical of Peking's new approach, Chiao Kuan-hua's 26 September 1975 address before the United Nations sharply rebutted Soviet claims of an "irreversible process of détente." Chiao stressed the enhanced danger of a "new world war" stemming from the U.S.-Soviet world rivalry, reiterating a recent Peking formulation that "whether war gives rise to revolution or revolution prevents war," the future will be "bright." (The previous year, by contrast, Chiao had stressed the then-prevalent PRC view that revolution, not superpower war, was the "main" international trend.) The foreign minister showed special concern over "deceptive" Soviet détente propaganda following the 1975 Helsinki summit on European security, bluntly warning that "it would be dangerous indeed" to "be so naive as to believe in the Soviet propaganda." Chiao designated the Soviet Union as the major threat to peace, asserting for the first time in authoritative Chinese comment that "the danger of war comes mainly from the wildly ambitious social imperialism."

Peking's antidétente view was underlined by a 1975 year-end comment which dwelt on Soviet "expansion" against the West under the cover of détente and disarmament. A 25 December 1975 *People's Daily* article by Jen Ku-ping flatly called the USSR "the most dangerous source of war," in contrast to a similar review of 1974 which had labeled both superpowers equally as potential sources of war. The article also departed from the 1974 comment's more evenhanded critique of the policies of both the USSR and the United States to scathingly denounce Moscow's strategy while softpedaling past charges against Washington.

Foreign Trade

The evolution of Chinese foreign trade policy has paralleled the general course of PRC foreign policy. Thus, for example, Chinese foreign trade was adversely affected by the ideological fervor evident in Chinese foreign policy during the Cultural Revolution. Political considerations sharply limited foreign trade options, to a point where China refused to trade with a number of foreign governments simply because those governments followed certain policies not in accord with Maoist ideology.

In the early 1970s, as Chou En-lai exerted increasing influence in the conduct of Chinese foreign affairs, China adopted a much more open approach to foreign trade. Peking began a pragmatic search for the best price in selling its goods abroad, and it tried to purchase the best foreign technology available, regardless of the political leanings of the country of origin. The Chinese began purchasing whole plants and inviting foreign experts to China to supervise their construction—a sharp departure from China's approach during the Cultural Revolution when foreign experts had been expelled from China or arrested as "spies."

The growth of leftist influence in Chinese foreign policy in 1974 again complicated the development of China's foreign trade. In late 1974 Peking cancelled a series of major orders for U.S. products. A number of leftist propaganda organs, especially the Shanghai journal *Study and Criticism,* had seriously questioned the benefits for China from increased foreign trade. The leftists criticized the arguments of Chou En-lai and the moderates that China should increase foreign trade in order to obtain the technology and materials needed to rapidly expand China's economic power and national welfare. The leftists complained that such policies went against Maoist teachings stressing the need for "self-reliance" and "independence" in China's economic development. They also charged that such policies would make China economically dependent on the United States and other major capitalist countries.

Major counterattacks by the moderates against leftist criticism of China's foreign trade policy in 1974 came in Teng Hsiao-ping's 10 April 1974 address before the UN

General Assembly's special session on economic affairs and in an article by Foreign Trade Minister Li Chiang which was publicized by NCNA on 9 July. Teng adopted a generally moderate position on all international economic issues discussed in his address. He lauded the Arab use of the oil weapon during the Middle East war as a model for third world struggles, and broadly supported moves to safeguard political independence and sovereignty over resources. He took a more moderate stand than some speakers by avoiding a blanket call for nationalization, but asserted support for steps to control foreign influence "up to and including nationalization." He also stated that developing countries should only "gradually" shake off control of foreign capital. Teng assumed a flexible attitude toward the role of trade and foreign exchange—subjects of debate within the Chinese leadership. He stuck to Peking's stress on self-reliance, but affirmed at the same time the Chinese belief that this in no way meant "self-seclusion" or rejection of foreign exchanges on an equitable basis.

Li Chiang's article calling for expanded PRC trade came in a new Chinese quarterly journal, *China's Foreign Trade*. Li indirectly countered leftist charges against China's foreign trade which had been pressed in 1974 during the campaign against Confucius and Lin Piao. Li claimed that the movement to criticize Lin and Confucius "will certainly promote" economic growth and result in increased foreign trade. Li also affirmed that "China's foreign trade is sound and reliable."

While Li's article gave due attention to the traditional Chinese principles of economic independence and self-reliance, he stressed that these principles "under no circumstances" meant pursuing a "closed door policy." Li went on to cite a comment Mao had made in 1949 concerning China's desire for expanded foreign trade, and noted the economic and political benefits China had derived from foreign trade since then. The article highlighted the "substantial" future potential in Peking's foreign trade because of China's "vast territory, rich resources, large population, and flourishing socialist construction," and stated that trade must develop "in steady steps."

Following Chou En-lai's death in January 1976 and the subsequent rise of leftist influence during the major political campaign to criticize Teng Hsiao-ping, there were revived harsh attacks on the moderates' foreign trade policies. The resurgence of the leftist anti-foreign trade line was vividly demonstrated in Chinese comment at the time of the spring 1976 Canton trade fair. NCNA comment marking the 15 May closing of the fair criticized Teng's "slavish comprador" foreign trade policy and gave unusual stress to the primacy of the principles of independence and self-reliance on China's national economic development. NCNA reaffirmed China's continued interest in importing foreign goods "in a planned way" but, unlike comment on fair closings in 1975, the propaganda did not advocate that China learn from foreigners, cater to foreign tastes in the manufacture and shipping of Chinese exports, or increase its foreign trade.

A 16 May NCNA commentary on the Canton fair's closing stressed the primary importance of Mao's line on "keeping to the principles of independence and self-reliance" while trading with foreign nations on the basis of the principles of "equality and mutual benefit." Another NCNA report on the 15th also emphasized that the number and quality of Chinese goods on display at the fair vividly demonstrated the rewards of China's adhering to self-reliance. By contrast, NCNA commentaries on the fair closings in November and May 1975 had given only passing attention to the need for independence and self-reliance. The 1975 comment had called on Chinese workers to seek the guidance of foreigners in order to improve the quality and value of China's exports, hailed the "remarkable changes" made in China's export trade, and flatly asserted that "China's foreign trade will continue to increase"—themes absent this time. The current comment did caution that China's stress on self-reliance did not mean that "we lock our door against the world and refuse to develop foreign trade or to introduce from abroad certain techniques and equipment really useful to China." NCNA claimed defensively that the present policy was "entirely different" from that advocated by Teng Hsiao-ping, which it said "depended on foreign techniques and equipment in developing China's economy so as to make imperialism and social imperialism gain control of the development of China's economy and reduce China to their economic appendage." It added that Teng had opposed the principles of independence and self-reliance, and had pushed a philosophy of "servility to things foreign" and the doctrine of "trailing behind at a snail's pace."

Following Hua Kuo-feng's purge of leftist leaders in October 1976, Peking quickly repudiated the leftist approach and reemphasized China's strong interest in developing trade abroad. NCNA comment on the opening of the Canton trade fair on 15 October 1976—immediately after the arrest of the leftist Chinese Politburo leaders—gave unusual stress to the importance of increasing China's foreign trade. It repeatedly cited Mao's 1949 injunction to expand international trade in order to promote Chinese production and economic prosperity.

A greater emphasis on foreign trade was reflected in NCNA coverage of meetings in Peking between Chinese officials and foreigners who were stopping off in the capital on their way to the Canton fair. In contrast to past years when NCNA had routinely noted only the atmosphere of such meetings, the agency stated explicitly that trade matters were discussed during the recent sessions. Thus, for example, NCNA on 14 October reported that Foreign Trade Minister Li Chiang had "exchanged views on the development of trade" during a talk that day with an Italian government delegation, and the agency on the same day noted that Vice Foreign Trade Minister Chai Shu-fan had exchanged views with a visiting Swedish delegation on "trade contacts."

A 9 October NCNA commentary announcing that the Canton fair was ready to open and a 15 October NCNA report of remarks at receptions marking the formal opening of the fair gave more attention than in past years to the importance of promoting wide-ranging trade contacts in order to improve China's economy and strengthen its influence abroad. Both contained an injunction of Mao's—not seen since 1974—stating that "the Chinese people wish to have friendly cooperation with the people of all countries and to resume and expand international trade in order to develop production and promote economic prosperity." NCNA on the 15th noted that Chinese officials speaking at the Canton reception had duly mentioned the principles of "independence and self-reliance" in Chinese economic development, but it gave much more stress to their statements of resolve "to run the current fair still better and make new contributions in further developing our country's foreign trade."

Chronology

1966

August   Lin Piao emerges as Mao's right-hand man. Red Guards appear for the first time.

September   NCNA says that Lin Piao is Mao's "intimate comrade in arms," and that Chiang Ching is deputy head of the Cultural Revolution group.

October   Soviet Premier Kosygin criticizes China for not adhering to the Soviet bloc's policy on Vietnam.

November   Mao reviews several million Red Guards in Peking.

1967

June   The Indian and Burmese embassies are besieged by demonstrators in Peking.

August   A coup is reported in the Chinese Foreign Ministry. Red Guards burn British diplomatic offices in Peking.

1968

May
Nepal's foreign minister visits China; peaceful coexistence is stressed during the visit.

August
A large outpouring of anti-Soviet polemics follows the Soviet invasion of Czechoslovakia.

November
Chinese Foreign Ministry calls for talks with the Nixon administration.

1969

February
China cancels talks with the Nixon administration.

March
Sino-Soviet clashes take place along the Ussuri River.

April
The Ninth Chinese Communist Party Congress meets.

May
Chinese ambassadors begin to return to their posts abroad.

August
Large-scale Sino-Soviet clash takes place along the Sinkiang border.

September
Soviet and Chinese premiers meet in Peking.

October
China entertains high-level visitors from

	North Vietnam, Cambodia, and North Korea.
	Sino-Soviet border talks begin in Peking.
November	China and Yugoslavia agree to resume ambassadorial-level relations.

1970

January	Sino-American talks resume in Warsaw.
April	Chou En-lai visits North Korea.
May	Mao Tse-tung condemns the U.S. incursion into Cambodia. The U.S.-PRC talks in Warsaw are suspended.
July	Chou En-lai calls for the formation of a broad international front against the two "superpowers."

1971

April	Chou En-lai greets a U.S. table tennis team visiting China.
July	Henry Kissinger makes a secret trip to China. President Nixon's forthcoming trip is announced.
September	Lin Piao reportedly dies in a plane crash in Mongolia.

October	The United Nations votes to accept the PRC and to expel Taiwan.

1972

February	President Nixon visits China, signs the Shanghai Communiqué.
September	Japanese Prime Minister Tanaka visits China, establishes diplomatic relations.

1973

January	The Paris peace agreement on Vietnam is signed.
February	The United States and China agree to establish liaison offices in Peking and Washington. China calls for peace talks with Taiwan.
August	The Tenth Chinese Communist Party Congress is held.

1974

January	A major transfer of Chinese military region commanders is reported. PRC forces assert China's claim to the Paracel Islands by driving out the South Vietnamese forces there.
February	Shrill propaganda marks a major upsurge

in the political campaign to criticize Confucius and Lin Piao.

March   A Soviet helicopter and its three man crew
             are captured in Sinkiang.

March-July   The campaign against Confucius and Lin
             Piao is accompanied by unusually stri-
             dent propaganda attacks against the Soviet
             Union, the United States, Japan, Taiwan,
             and other countries.

1975

January   The Fourth National People's Congress
             meets in Peking.

March-April Communist forces are victorious against
             U.S.-supported regimes in Cambodia and
             Vietnam.

June   Philippines President Marcos visits China,
             establishes diplomatic relations.

July   Thailand's prime minister visits China,
             establishes diplomatic relations.

September   Vietnam's national day is marked by signs
             of cooling in Sino-Vietnamese relations.

             China's foreign minister sharply attacks
             U.S.-Soviet détente and for the first time
             labels the Soviet Union as the most danger-
             ous source of war.

November   Peking media criticize the dismissal of U.S.
                Defense Secretary Schlesinger.

December   President Ford visits China.

                Peking announces the return of the Soviet
                helicopter and crew captured in 1974.

1976

January   Chou En-lai dies.

February   Hua Kuo-feng is named acting premier;
                Teng Hsiao-ping drops from public view.

September   Mao Tse-tung dies.

October   Four leftist Chinese Politburo members are
                arrested. Hua Kuo-feng is named chairman
                of the CCP.

1977

January   Leader of Bangladesh visits China, con-
                cludes agreement on economic aid and
                mutual trade.

                Peking blames Moscow for deadlock in
                their border talks, and labels the USSR as
                "the most dangerous source of new war"
                and as harboring a "sinister intention to
                control and enslave Asian countries."

Bibliography

Barnett, A. Doak. *Uncertain Passage. China's Transition to the Post-Mao Era.* Washington: The Brookings Institution, 1974.

Brown, Roger Glenn. "Chinese Politics and American Policy." *Foreign Policy* 23 (1976): 3-23.

Bridgham, Philip. "Mao's Cultural Revolution: The Struggle to Seize Power." *China Quarterly* 41 (1970): 1-25.

Bulletin of Atomic Scientists. *China After the Cultural Revolution.* New York: Random House, 1970.

Chay, John, ed. *The Problems and Prospects of American–East Asian Relations.* Boulder, Colorado: Westview Press, 1976.

Clubb, O. Edmund. *China and Russia: The Great Game.* New York: Columbia University Press, 1970.

Clough, Ralph N. *East Asia and U.S. Security.* Washington: The Brookings Institution, 1975.

Clough, Ralph N. *The United States, China, and Arms Control.* Washington: The Brookings Institution, 1975.

Endicott, John E., and William R. Heaton. *The Politics of East Asia.* Boulder, Colorado: Westview Press, 1978.

Fitzgerald, Stephen. *China and the Overseas Chinese: A Study of Peking's Changing Policy, 1949-1970.* Cambridge: Cambridge University Press, 1972.

Freidman, Edward, and Mark Selden, eds. *America's Asia.* New York: Pantheon Books, 1971.

Gittings, John. "The Great Power Triangle and Chinese Foreign Policy." *China Quarterly* 39 (1969): 41-54.

Gittings, John. *The World and China.* New York: Harper and Row, 1974.

Gutov, Melvin. "The Foreign Ministry and Foreign Affairs during the Cultural Revolution." *China Quarterly* 40 (1969): 65-102.

Hellmann, Donald C., ed. *China and Japan: A New Balance of Power.* Lexington, Mass.: Lexington Books, 1976.

Hinton, Harold C. *China's Turbulent Quest.* New York: Macmillan, 1970.

Hinton, Harold C. *Bear at the Gate: Chinese Policymaking Under Soviet Pressure.* Washington: American Enterprise Institute for Public Policy Research, 1971.

Hinton, Harold C. *Three and a Half Powers: The New Balance in Asia.* Bloomington: Indiana University Press, 1975.

Moorstein, Richard, and Morton Abramowitz. *Remaking China Policy: U.S.-China Relations and Governmental Decisionmaking.* Cambridge: Harvard University Press, 1971.

Mozingo, David. *China's Foreign Policy and the Cultural Revolution.* Ithaca, N.Y.: Cornell University Press, 1970.

Pillsbury, Michael. "U.S.-China Military Ties?" *Foreign Policy* 20 (1975): 50-64.

Scalapino, Robert. *Asia and the Road Ahead: Issues for the Major Powers.* Berkeley: University of California Press, 1975.

Scalapino, Robert. "The Dragon, the Tiger, and the Wolf—Sino-Soviet Relations and Their Impact on Asia," Orbis 19 (1975): 838-862.

Terrill, Ross. *The 800 Million.* Boston: Little, Brown, and Co., 1972.

Terrill, Ross. *Flowers on an Iron Tree: Five Cities of China.* Boston: Atlantic Monthly Press, 1975.

Van Ness, Peter. *Revolution and Chinese Foreign Policy: Peking's Support for Wars of National Liberation.* Berkeley: University of California Press, 1970.

Whiting, Allen. "The Use of Force in Foreign Policy by the People's Republic of China." *The Annals* (July 1972): 55-66.

Whiting, Allen. *The Chinese Calculus of Deterrence: India and Indochina.* Ann Arbor: University of Michigan Press, 1975.

Wich, Richard. "Chinese Allies and Adversaries." In *The Military and Political Power of China in the 1970s,* edited by William W. Whitson. New York: Praeger Publishers, 1972.

Wilcox, Francis O., ed. *China and the Great Powers: Relations with the United States, the Soviet Union, and Japan.* New York: Praeger Publishers, 1974.

Index